PRAISE FOR PAUL KUSSEROW
AND *THE ANATOMY OF A TURNAROUND*

Lessons that will not only cultivate better business leaders but also nurture better human beings.

—from the Foreword by **SENATOR BILL FRIST, MD**, former Majority Leader of the US Senate

Paul Kusserow's turnaround of Amedisys is legendary within the healthcare industry. But the lessons in this book are broadly applicable for anyone contemplating taking on an impossible job, fraught with risk, on which many are depending and for which the stakes are extremely high.

—**TREVOR FETTER**, Senior Lecturer of Business Administration at Harvard Business School and former Chairman and CEO of Tenet Healthcare Corporation

Paul has been the leading voice in Washington for care in the home. This book chronicles not only the transformation of an amazing Baton Rouge–based company, but the necessity of driving more of our care out of institutions and into the home.

—**SENATOR BILL CASSIDY, MD**

During my time running CMS, Paul was a tireless advocate for driving more care into the home. He was right. His book explains why.

—**SEEMA VERMA**, former Administrator of the Centers for Medicare and Medicaid Services

A true innovator, Paul sees things others don't. *The Anatomy of a Turnaround* is about using basic principles that engage all in the act of caregiving and creating enormous value by tapping into that energy.

—**ADAM BOEHLER**, CEO of Rubicon Founders Opportunity Fund and former Director of the Center for Medicare and Medicaid Innovation (CMMI)

Paul ran strategy for Humana during the last five years of my tenure as CEO. His vision, passion, and ability to innovate within the company and push us forward were extraordinary and key to helping us transform ourselves into the company we are today. His insightful book helps us understand the elements of transformative company building.

—**MICHAEL McCALLISTER**, Chairman of Zoetis and former Chairman and CEO of Humana

It's refreshing to see someone who relentlessly pushes a company to do what it should be doing: serving its people, so they can serve the customers. In services, it's all about the people and structuring an environment where employees can be at their best. To illustrate the mechanics of implementing his Golden Rule leadership principles, Paul details the four stages of Amedisys's transformation. As a CEO myself, I've benefited from Paul's philosophies as applied to both my business and personal lives. I'm sure readers will feel the same way after finishing Paul's insightful and entertaining book.

—**MIKE PYKOSZ**, Chairman and CEO of Oak Street Health

Paul is a force. His book is, too. He studies and learns from all angles, develops market-based strategies, divides the work so everyone has a piece, and then tracks relentlessly until he hits his goals. The results of this method have produced some amazing results.

—**SEAN SLOVENSKI**, CEO of Avēsis Corporation and former
President of Walmart Health

As a former CEO and leadership advisor to the top healthcare CEOs in the world, I've seen firsthand what it takes to lead through transformation. Paul is one of the best, and his transformation of Amedisys is an incredible story. By aligning the business mission to a passion for serving the most vulnerable and combining his business acumen with uncompromising execution, Paul has become a uniquely successful CEO. This book describes how you can take that journey as well.

—**SARAH LADD EAMES**, Managing Director at Russell Reynolds
and Associates, cofounder of Roundtable for Healthcare CEOs,
and former CEO of Allied Healthcare International

Paul's courageous moves in Amedisys's early days—focusing on a few key things, rigorously tracking and measuring progress, and moving the fly wheel—showed what grit and intense strategic focus can do to drive operational performance.

—**JON KAPLAN**, Managing Director and Senior Partner at
Boston Consulting Group

Paul is passionate and deeply knowledgeable, with an incredible sense of how things should be. He is one of the key people I turn to when trying to figure out where the puck is going. *The Anatomy of a Turnaround* outlines the orientation future seekers and change makers need to adopt to be transformative.

—**ROBB VORHOFF**, Managing Director and Global Head of
Healthcare at General Atlantic LLC

Paul is one of the most original, broad-reaching minds I've encountered in the healthcare world. *The Anatomy of a Turnaround* is a fascinating study of how to transform healthcare and how to do it in an inclusive, empowering way for all.

—**JONATHAN KOLSTAD**, Henry J. Kaiser Chair at the Haas Business School of the University of California, Berkeley, and Director of The Center for Healthcare at UC Berkeley Opportunity Lab

Paul and I worked together at Humana and have remained close personally and professionally throughout the years. Like many others, I have benefited greatly from his support and informed counsel. He is a visionary. At Humana and elsewhere, Paul has driven transformation that created real and lasting value. His insights here serve as a testament and guide to driving compassionate, people-oriented leadership.

—**KEN FASOLA**, President of Centene Corporation

KKR took a risk when we brought in a relatively untested strategist to lead the Amedisys turnaround. We believed in Paul's intellect, his passion for building culture and for helping people. Boy, did he deliver! Amedisys was an outstanding investment for KKR. For me personally, participating in the extraordinary turnaround of Amedisys is one of the proudest moments of my business career. Paul is a terrific leader and even better person. His book tells our story of going all in on principled leadership.

—**NAT ZILKHA**, cofounder and Executive Chairman of Firebird Music Holdings, Chairman of Gibson Brands, and former Partner at KKR Credit

Paul and I spent many days on the road together during our time with The Advisory Board. His deep knowledge of healthcare and how it works, coupled with his passion for change and transformation, has made him one of the leading thinkers in healthcare today.

—**ERIC LARSEN**, President of Advisory Board

Smart as heck, passionate, unrelenting, true to his vision, and irrepressible. Paul finally got his own show at Amedisys and proved the principles of compassion, the democratization of healthcare, service, and selfless attention to your constituencies and, specifically, to the customer experience will drive performance off the charts.

—**RALPH JUDAH**, former Senior Managing Director at Deloitte

When Paul came along and showed the world what care in the home was and what it could be and should be, things changed. This book is a testament to how Paul helped transform our perceptions of home care.

—**BRIAN TANQUILIT**, Healthcare Services Equity Research Analyst
    at Jefferies

I always try to have Paul lecture to my graduate classes each year. His framing and approach are unique. More importantly, however, they're practical, memorable, and highly relatable to my students. They are struck by the CEO's commitment to meet thousands of his company's associates nationwide as a foundational exercise to understand the organization's potential. Paul's results speak to the honest but hard work of listening to your markets and delivering value to your constituents. This book outlines how doing the right thing can lead to exceptional results.

—**LARRY VAN HORN, PHD**, Associate Professor of Management
    (Economics), Associate Professor of Law, and Executive Director
    for Health Affairs at Vanderbilt University and Director of the
    Center for Healthcare Market Innovation Research

THE
ANATOMY
OF A
TURNAROUND

THE
ANATOMY
OF A
TURNAROUND

TRANSFORMING AN ORGANIZATION BY PRIORITIZING PEOPLE, PERFORMANCE, AND PURPOSE

PAUL KUSSEROW

Mc
Graw
Hill

NEW YORK CHICAGO SAN FRANCISCO ATHENS LONDON
MADRID MEXICO CITY MILAN NEW DELHI
SINGAPORE SYDNEY TORONTO

1 2 3 4 5 6 7 8 9   LCR   28 27 26 25 24 23

ISBN   978-1-265-49981-5
MHID   1-265-49981-0

e-ISBN   978-1-265-50061-0
e-MHID   1-265-50061-4

Library of Congress Cataloging-in-Publication Data
Names: Kusserow, Paul, author.
Title: The anatomy of a turnaround : transforming an organization by
    prioritizing people, performance, and positioning / Paul Kusserow.
Description: New York : McGraw Hill, [2024] | Includes bibliographical
    references and index.
Identifiers: LCCN 2023008792 (print) | LCCN 2023008793 (ebook) |
    ISBN 9781265499815 (hardback) | ISBN 9781265500610 (ebook)
Subjects: LCSH: Kusserow, Paul. | Health services administration—United
    States. | Home care services—United States—Administration. |
    Organizational change.
Classification: LCC RA971 .K87 2024 (print) | LCC RA971 (ebook) |
    DDC 362.14—dc23/eng/20230527
LC record available at https://lccn.loc.gov/2023008792
LC ebook record available at https://lccn.loc.gov/2023008793

McGraw Hill books are available at special quantity discounts to use as premiums and sales promotions or for use in corporate training programs. To contact a representative, please visit the Contact Us pages at www.mhprofessional.com.

McGraw Hill is committed to making our products accessible to all learners. To learn more about the available support and accommodations we offer, please contact us at accessibility@mheducation.com. We also participate in the Access Text Network (www.accesstext.org), and ATN members may submit requests through ATN.

For Serena,
always

For everything there is a season,
and a time for every purpose under heaven

—Ecclesiastes 3:1–8

CONTENTS

FOREWORD

I first met Paul Kusserow shortly after completing my two-term tenure in the US Senate, the last four years as Majority Leader. Having spent 20 years previously in clinical medicine as a heart and lung transplant surgeon, I was now freshly embarking upon an exciting third career, as an investor and partner with my friend Bryan Cressey at his healthcare private equity firm, Cressey and Company.

I had heard Paul's name sprinkled around in various conversations as I was getting settled and establishing myself in the private investment world. My new partner, Bryan, somewhat of a legacy in his own right, spoke enthusiastically of Paul as a highly creative and original healthcare thinker with whom he liked to trade ideas. Paul's name kept coming up again and again as I sought out the best and the brightest to learn from, so I was intrigued to meet him.

During the second week of January each year, there is an annual migration of healthcare companies, entrepreneurs, thought and policy leaders all converging in San Francisco for the JPMorgan Conference. It's an exhilarating and exhausting whirlwind of a week, a bit of a cattle call but always worth the time and energy spent. The event enables investors like us, within a week's timeframe, to efficiently see a huge number of people, to hear and share emerging trends and ideas in the healthcare market, to meet with companies we want to know or consider for investment now or later, to follow up on the progress of companies we are tracking or invested in, as well as to connect with influencers and thought leaders.

The Cressey team hosted meetings and interviews at the same venue every year. It's not far from the main conference site at the St. Francis Hotel on Union Square. More action happens outside and around the St. Francis than inside. Investors, like us, schedule hundreds of back-to-back meetings, attend seminars, host networking dinners, learn about current industry trends, evaluate upcoming company leaders, search for investment opportunities, and touch base and engage with thought leaders. JPM gets the new business year off to a fast start and sets the stage for much of the year's subsequent deal flow.

As I looked at my schedule, I saw that Bryan had arranged for the two of us to have an hour-long meeting with Paul. That was highly unusual. Bryan and I had agreed to a "divide and conquer" approach to scheduling meetings during JPM. We wanted to use our limited time efficiently. Most meetings were short, some just a half-hour. I was new to private equity but realized that an hour was a long time for the firm's leaders to spend with a single individual whom we weren't recruiting or doing a deal with. I asked Bryan why this particular meeting was so important. He responded, "Paul is well worth the time. We share perspectives and compare ideas. He's uniquely knowledgeable. Trust me. You'll see."

So we met with Paul, and Bryan was right. As the then-head of strategy, business development, and innovations for Humana, Paul's observations on the current state of the health sector triggered a fascinating, wide-ranging, no-holds-barred discussion of people, companies, and trends. Paul's work at Humana was groundbreaking and innovative. He recognized Medicare Advantage's potential to grow

Humana's footprint and revenues. He was pushing the company hard to become the industry leader in MA. At the same time, Paul was acquiring companies and quickly assembling internal capabilities to develop care management expertise, a prerequisite for running a profitable MA business. With relentless persistence, he drove Humana into value-based care well ahead of other major health insurers.

Paul jokingly labeled himself Humana's "intrapreneur," someone who could innovate from inside a company, even one as large and complex as Humana. Paul's vast experience and unique perspective were important to Cressey as we refined our investment thesis to embrace value-based care ourselves and as we tried to decipher what would be realistically adopted in the markets and what was too far in the future. Paul gave us color and substance.

That was the beginning of a long and enriching friendship. Our annual JPM visits continued. We often exchanged notes and shared investment ideas. Despite our consistent contact, in 2015, I was surprised when Paul called for advice on where to live in Nashville, my hometown.

Paul had left his comfortable corporate strategy job at Humana and jumped into a full-blown turnaround at Amedisys, one of the industry's leading home care companies. Paul was in the process of moving Amedisys's executive functions from the company's headquarters in Baton Rouge to Nashville. The company needed a deeper and more diverse talent pool than the one that was available in Louisiana.

Paul also wanted Amedisys to become a major component of Nashville's robust healthcare ecosystem. He rightly thought Nashville was the nation's mecca for healthcare services. Paul believed he and his senior leadership team would experience the region's tremendous healthcare depth and diversity by engaging with companies at all stages of development across the wide healthcare continuum that is uniquely in Nashville. He thought Amedisys needed to stretch its thinking, play on a bigger stage, and strive to shape, in partnership with others, healthcare's brave new world. There was and is no place better than Nashville to realize Paul's bold vision for Amedisys.

When Paul moved to Nashville, we saw each other regularly. He immediately immersed himself into the vibrant healthcare community and culture. I invited Paul to become a guest on my popular *A Second Opinion* podcast. Prior to the show, we did research on the Amedisys turnaround. What the company had accomplished under his leadership was amazing. Beyond reinvigorating the company's financials, Paul had elevated the industry's appreciation for the long-neglected home care sector. He knew for certain that care for America's aging population was going to shift from institutions into the home because it was what consumers wanted, it generated better outcomes, and it cost much less money. He saw where it was all heading and had smartly positioned Amedisys to capitalize on this massive opportunity.

Considering his background in strategy, it's not surprising that Paul recognized the trend toward home care earlier than others. What impressed me was how he turned that vision into reality. Strategists rarely excel at operations. Paul is an exception. As its CEO, he transformed Amedisys from a stagnant provider of low-skill care services into a dynamic growth company leading a revitalized and reimagined home care industry. The company's stock price surged. Everyone now understood the immense value of being able to provide quality care in the home.

Even more remarkable than Amedisys's superb financial and operational performance is the manner in which Paul achieved these results. Instead of dictating the company's strategic direction from on high, he listened, inviting Amedisys's caregivers, operators, and patients to help define, refine, and execute the company's strategy. He shared with me how, in his first three months as CEO, he went on the road, visiting 34 care centers in 17 states, talking to patients, care-givers, administrators, office staff, referral sources, those that liked Amedisys, and those that didn't. In my experience, though many talk about it, very few CEOs actually take the time to intimately meet with and understand all those involved in and touched by their orga-nization. But Paul did, and he did it with true compassion and con-viction. Through this process of patient- and employee-led strategy, Amedisys rediscovered its passion and capability for providing great care, allowing it to burst forth from within. Patients responded and the business grew. Unlocking untapped human potential generates unmatched investment returns, which is what Paul had set out to prove. People- and culture-centered change saved Amedisys and transformed the company into a home care juggernaut.

This is not your typical book about top-down, command-and-control, CEO-as-hero leadership. Paul digs deep to reveal how human beings manifest their best selves by serving others. Treating employees well means they pay it back and go the extra mile for patients. The company prospers from everyone's collective efforts, all directed toward giving great care to patients.

Paul's background and training in theology, philosophy, psychol-ogy, and literature encouraged him to use novel, human-centered approaches to drive transformation. His central leadership tenets are unique: serve employees so they can serve customers, listen to the marketplace for guidance, invest from the core outward, open the company and its strategy to all stakeholders, find the answers to tough challenges inside the company, stage transformation systemat-ically, find hidden value in discarded or overlooked investments, cele-brate employees when they leave, and most importantly, Golden Rule management practices always and everywhere. Treat others the way you want to be treated. Or as Paul says, "Treat everyone like they are your mom." These strategies work. Look at the results.

Paul's informative, insightful, and entertaining narrative engages readers and teaches us principles that transcend business. Following his lessons will not only cultivate better business leaders but also nurture better human beings. As Paul told me, "I've become a better person by being a caregiver—learning to lead by serving, listening, and enabling." It is fascinating to follow Paul's journey throughout *The Anatomy of a Turnaround*. I hope that more companies will employ his principles to achieve Amedisys-like success for their organizations.

SENATOR BILL FRIST, MD

Former Majority Leader of the US Senate, founding Partner of Frist Cressey Ventures, and Special Partner of Cressey and Company

INTRODUCTION

Seeking Truth

I have an unusual background and a set of beliefs informed by the study of theology, philosophy, and literature as well as numerous and diverse career stops in multiple industries. This book not only chronicles Amedisys's successful turnaround and repositioning. It also incorporates life and leadership lessons that I learned on my way to the corner office. These hard-earned lessons have molded me as an individual, citizen, and CEO.

By most objective accounts, I was a very successful CEO. During my first time in the Amedisys captain's chair, I helped reshape a company that was falling apart to one that is now thriving and leading the expansive home care industry. Turning the company around brought us into the national spotlight and elevated the importance of home-based care in advancing healing, patient-centric care, and value creation.

Across the board, the results the company has achieved during my tenure are by any measures extraordinary. You will get the specifics in the book, but here is what the company stated in the press release announcing my transition from CEO to chairman in April 2022:

Amedisys Under Paul Kusserow's Leadership

- Improved Home Health Quality of Patient Care Star scores from 3.5 Stars to 4.33 Stars—leading the industry
- Migrated the entire Amedisys business to the Homecare Homebase (HCHB) platform
- Focused on employees and being the Employer of Choice resulting in a voluntary turnover rate of approximately 18 percent and landing Amedisys on Modern Healthcare's Best Place to Work list in 2021
- Expanded Amedisys's lines of business from Home Health and Hospice to Home Health, Hospice, Personal Care, Palliative Care, Hospital at Home and Skilled Nursing Facility (SNF) at Home
- Invested in the Hospice business growing census from approximately 4,600 to over 13,000 and increasing the number of care centers from 80 to 177
- Expanded consolidated adjusted EBITDA margin from approximately 6 percent to over 13 percent
- Grew the market cap of Amedisys from $750 million to over $5.3 billion generating substantial shareholder value

I am organically wired to fix things. The status quo is never quite good enough. This penchant for relentless improvement often makes me a difficult colleague. I was decades into my professional career before learning this about myself. Here's how it happened.

Between 1997 and 2004, I was the chief strategy officer for Tenet Healthcare, the nation's second largest for-profit hospital system. As

I was ending my tenure at the company, Tenet's CEO, my friend and mentor, Trevor Fetter, asked what I wanted as a farewell gift. A remarkable gesture, Trevor's generosity made an enormous difference in both my personal and my business life thereafter.

As I was deciding what to request, I wrote two fictional obituaries. I was at a crossroads in my journey, and I had read that writing comparative obituaries was an effective way to assess one's life and career. The first assumed I had accomplished everything I wanted in life. The second assumed I got hit by a bus and died that day. The contrast was brutal. This exercise, albeit a bit corny, was very revealing.

What I had been doing was not getting me anywhere close to where I wanted to go or what I wanted to be. In fact, much of what I was doing was taking me in the opposite direction. I was on my way to becoming like Kurtz, the main character in Joseph Conrad's *Heart of Darkness*. On his deathbed, Kurtz realizes that he is a hollow man as he recounts the moral lies he's told himself to justify his illicit actions. His final words are, "The horror! The horror!" I was in my early forties, and I did not want that future.

I had checked the boxes everywhere else, though. I had a wonderful family. My wife, Serena, was the best partner I could imagine. Our three daughters were happy and healthy. We lived in a beautiful old hacienda in the middle of a lemon orchard overlooking the Pacific Ocean. But at the same time, I didn't feel that my work either suited me or was meaningful. Like Kurtz, I had good excuses for my choices. My career funded the other things that made my family's life so good. I equated much of my career decision-making to money—having enough of it, so there would be security in my life. That rationale, however, was complete nonsense. I had already made "my number." Like a squirrel preparing for an endless winter, I kept maniacally foraging for income in unhappy places and frenetically packing it away. With this Kurtz-like mindset, there would never be enough.

Writing the obituaries made me realize that I was unhappy with my career's progress and unenthusiastic about its future trajectory. I wondered what I would do for the next 30 years with my professional life. I needed to feel like the time and effort I was putting forth were noble and worthwhile even if I didn't achieve all my goals. At a minimum, I wanted to be heading in the right direction.

I had to understand why I'd made the choices I had, why I was stuck in jobs that I didn't particularly like, why I worked with people I found distasteful. It was time for a change. This sobering realization drove me to ask Trevor to send me to a professional development program at Harvard Business School. He agreed, and I headed off to Cambridge for a week that would change my life.

As part of the program, I met several times with Jim Waldroop, a trained psychologist. Jim helped aspiring and mid-career executives increase their professional self-awareness and choose careers suited to their skills and cognitive orientation. Under Jim's guidance, I completed multiple cognitive assessment tools and developmental exercises. They were fun and interesting. As the week progressed, he asked lots of questions and listened to my responses.

I called Dr. Waldroop my "career shrink." On the last day of the program, Jim delivered his conclusions. He had patiently listened to my spoiled whining and agonizing as I struggled to define my place in the world. His answer was simple. He said, "You're a seeker," and then made the following observations about seekers' peculiar orientation and their consequential impact:

You're never going to be happy or satisfied with the status quo. You're always going to push the boundaries of things because you believe everything, including yourself, has yet to find its true potential. You want more and more because you honestly believe there is more. You love the idea more than the reality, but you keep pushing your reality to become the ideal. That's the brutal truth about you.

If you're going to stay in business, you need to be the futurist in an organization that can afford the disruption that someone like you introduces into the ranks. All places want and need change, but few admit it. You'll best fit into the places that admit they really need and want change.

Some places want to hear about what they should be and where they need to get to, but change is hard. Most companies stick to the status quo as long as they possibly can. That's where you have been, and that's why you have become frustrated. Worse for you, most places are happy with where they are and spend a lot of time justifying it. Having someone like you in their ranks can be disruptive, even toxic . . .

You will be best working in an organization that is bent on or needs transformation or is creating the future, such as a startup or a fast-growth disruptor. Or you'll need to go into places that are on fire, busted, or near dead, which need to be repositioned or turned around—where you can find a new future for them and lead them to it.

You can lead at these places because there are very few people like you who love broken things and want to restore them. If you go big, you should go for broke and make sure you're the boss.

Never forget, though, that you are a seeker with a substantial amount of unrelenting will, energy, and intensity. As your companies evolve, there will be a demand for different skills and roles to be played—same stage, different script and players that will need to adapt to the new script. That applies to you too.

Be mindful that your seeking skills will bring organizations to the right place, by hook or by crook, but once they get there, you'll need to let them recover—allow them to settle into and acclimatize to their new world. Constant radical change is not a good thing for anything or anybody; it's not sustainable except maybe for someone like you.

Dr. Waldroop smiled broadly after making his last observation. This conversation with him was immensely helpful. His characterization of me made sense. Understanding that I was a seeker gave me revelatory context for my successes and failures. His framing answered my probing questions about myself and my future. It enabled me to better position myself for new roles and opportunities. From there, my career stops included startups and venture investing as well as strategy and innovation roles. My seeking eventually led me to Amedisys, a company that needed saving, which operated within an industry segment (home care) that required redefinition.

Working at Amedisys was an amazing and transformative experience. I tested and put into work ideas and concepts that I had long believed could enrich employees' daily work and turbocharge organizational performance. These beliefs shaped long-term strategies and on-the-spot decisions. My lens and methods are different from those of traditional corporate CEOs. Employing them led Amedisys to achieve extraordinary success. There's value in understanding how this occurred.

I'm a notetaker, always have been. At the end of each year, I buy the biggest, thickest Moleskine datebooks made, and then I write everything down in them. Like a third grader, I amuse myself by using different colored pens to write out the next day's meetings. I keep my colored pens in a bright orange pencil pouch that I bought at an Italian school supplies store while hiking in the Alps near Cortina. I literally create a colorful schedule for myself in the hope that it will lead to a colorful day. More days than not, the approach works. It gets me excited and engaged for whoever and whatever is coming next.

Within the datebook's calendar, there are two-page note sections that follow each week. I fill these sections with meeting notes, important facts, follow-ups, and to-dos, also in different colors. They become my memory. At the end of my notebook, following the last week of December, there are 33 blank pages. Over the years I have filled these pages as well, using the exercise of writing to work out thorny problems, think deeply about concepts, and jot insights as I work through various opportunities and situations. In general, my year-end pages contain significant ideas that transcend the weekly checklists. Like the tide relative to ocean waves, these pages guide my strategic thinking just as the checklists guide my daily activities.

More often than not, these year-end pages are a ragged, unfinished collage of thoughts that point to something meaningful but do not get fully there. They are very much like a junkman's backyard full of rows of cars on blocks. The junkman tells himself, "I'm going to get them running someday. They just need some parts or extra work to get them on the road." He sees each car's potential, but the cars progressively rust as the seasons pass. They become harder to fix. I try not to let my unfinished ideas rust but don't always succeed. The life of the mind is precious but fragile. I have about 15 notebooks and datebooks that cover my Amedisys journey.

In college I had a Pulitzer Prize–winning writing teacher who told me that there's nothing really new to say. There's not much about human nature that hasn't already been said multiple times. The question for each of us as individuals and leaders is how we apply established knowledge in ways that resonate with people, improve their understanding, ignite them in common purpose, and motivate them to act.

Writing forces thoroughness. It requires us to be cogent and analytical in a way conversation does not. In conversation, we can get away with undeveloped themes and threads of ideas. Good writing, as stated in Strunk and White's classic *Elements of Style*, creates whole, polished ideas that stand on their own. It rounds things off and makes ideas hold together. So I write to find meaning, discover new linkages, and become a better communicator. Writing is hard work. It forces me to string thoughts and concepts together until they become complete and whole. When an idea comes out clearly, complete, and fully rounded, there is nothing more fulfilling.

Writing this book has forced me to flesh out my ideas, clarify my thinking, eliminate the rust. I revisited my Amedisys notebooks, scoured them for useful ideas, and present the ideas with promise to readers. Round out the edges, locate the missing parts, fill in the holes, and see if they can leave the blocks.

I did not plan to write this book. Friends, colleagues, and thought leaders repeatedly asked me to articulate and share the ideas that had worked so successfully at Amedisys. After I stepped down as CEO, several of my fellow board members (I remained board chair) as well as my wife insisted that I chronicle the company's turnaround. I couldn't do that without simultaneously digging into my own background, experiences, successes, and failures. This book blends two transformations: my own and the company's. They could not have happened in isolation. They crisscross and intersect in innumerable ways. Transformation is not a straightforward endeavor. Surprise is inevitable. Joy and pain intermingle. Knowledge is hard-won. For these reasons, I think of myself as a scribe. I chronicle Amedisys's transformation from the CEO's perch, but I do so with the humble and profound realization that our people were the real change agents. They did the hard and necessary work. I just wrote it down.

In this spirit of common purpose, all book sale proceeds will go directly back to our caregivers and patients via the Amedisys Foundation. This is ultimately their story. They should gain any rewards that come from my telling it.

Being Amedisys's CEO as it pivoted toward greatness was the experience of a lifetime. That's rewarding enough for me. I can't wait to share this story with you. Let's get started.

1

A CEO MATCH MADE IN HEAVEN AND HELL

In December 2014, I became the CEO of a publicly traded healthcare company based in Baton Rouge, Louisiana, called Amedisys. At the time I was 53, and it was my first CEO job, pretty late by most standards.

I got the job because basically no potential CEOs worth their salt would take the position. The company was on the brink, toxic, and a real mess. Prior to my hiring, the board tried to give the company away for a song to one of our largest competitors. They refused the offer. Not being able to sell the company, the board was desperate to find a CEO willing to step into the role and try to reverse the company's fortunes. Six months after I'd completed a consulting engagement that led to the founder/CEO's resignation, after the company had run through all other options and prospective candidates, the board asked me if I would become Amedisys's new CEO.

Most people's idea of me at this time was pretty uniform. "Smart, quirky guy with an evangelical confidence in his ability to read the tea leaves. Overeducated with completely irrelevant knowledge for the business world. Hasn't met a futuristic idea or transformative strategy he doesn't love. Excellent on strategy, figuring out where the puck is going. Intuitive problem solver. Let him draw the company a road map. Let him help plan how to get there. Even let him do the deals to get the assets to achieve the vision. But in God's name, don't let him drive the car. Have Paul at the table to plan and strategize, cut/build/buy/do joint venture deals, poke and disrupt, pressure-test, and offer alternative ideas, but don't let him implement or operate anything. Look elsewhere for a CEO. Paul provides some nice frosting, but he's not the whole cake."

My relationship with Amedisys began with a consulting engagement. My good friend and mentor, David Pitts, was a longstanding senior member of the Amedisys board. Along with several other board members, David was becoming increasingly concerned about the company's direction. In early 2014, he called me on behalf of the board and asked me to take a look at the company's strategy. If there is one thing I can do well, it's strategy. I had just left a big strategy job at Humana and was working to get an innovative, next-generation off the ground. I wanted to help David and also thought the Amedisys engagement would be a good side gig while we were getting our startup planned and funded.

I brought in the consulting firm BCG to help dig into Amedisys's operations and competitive positioning. I had worked with BCG before and liked its analytical rigor and approach to problem solving. Our analysis ripped the company down to its studs. We found lots of strategic, cultural, organizational, and executional rot along the way. Bad sign—the deeper we dug, the worse things got. It took a lot of work to find solid ground. Fortunately, there was a core clinical foundation underneath the mounds of fluffery: Amedisys took good care of its patients.

In our presentation to the board, we highlighted that the company in its present state was teetering and unstable. We pinpointed the sources of rot and instability. These included strategic misalignment with market demands and the lack of core capabilities necessary to compete effectively in newly targeted markets. We detailed a grim scenario of what would happen if the company continued on its current trajectory. We then gave the board a series of detailed playbook binders outlining how to address critical issues and fix the company. I had gotten input and buy-in from many Amedisys leaders and frontline caregivers. Based on these conversations, I was confident that we had identified the right issues and come to the right conclusions.

I insisted that our Amedisys collaborators coauthor the final report with us, so it would be theirs too. If the company's existing leaders owned and implemented our recommendations, we believed Amedisys could recover and right itself quickly. David Pitts was ecstatic about our work, as were several other board members. The chairman/CEO/founder, Bill Borne, was not.

Before I go farther, I'd like to provide some background and perspective on Bill Borne. I was and continue to be a huge admirer and fan of Bill's. I particularly admire both the company he built and the way in which he built it. His bold entrepreneurialism and hands-on management made Amedisys a major player in the home care industry. The legacy he created during a legendary 30-year career are inspirational and worthy of singular recognition.

As was his prerogative as CEO, Bill disagreed strongly with our report's conclusions and strategic recommendations. He believed fervently that Amedisys should continue on the strategic path he had painstakingly engineered. During the consulting engagement, my interactions with Bill were bizarre. I flew out several times to meet with him and his direct reports in Baton Rouge. Bill had converted an old, cavernous, former regional, big-box grocery store called Schwegmann's into the company's headquarters. The executive offices sat behind a locked door that required a special passkey to enter.

The office arrangements spoke volumes about the corporate culture. Senior Amedisys execs came in through a separate entry. They had their own bathrooms, kitchen, food, and snack services. This executive facility housed a huge boardroom largely for the use of the CEO and his direct reports. As consultants, we knew the source of the company's power and influence resided in this executive facility. Accordingly, we located our office in a small windowless conference room adjacent to the boardroom.

Management consultants fight to the death to be near the sources of the company's power. If consultants aren't in dialogue with the CEO and his team, engagements tend to be short and unprofitable. A basic consulting strategy to win business and build a long-term client relationship is do the first study quickly and cheaply. Show value and make sure there are lots of follow-on questions that should be resolved by continued work. This approach gets your hooks into the client (preferably the CEO), builds a dependence, and sets the foundation for very profitable follow-on work. The key to cementing a long-term consulting arrangement is establishing regular dialogue with CEOs and their teams. Loyalty and dependence follow.

Bill knew things were not going well, but it was his company and he had been at the helm since the beginning, over 30 years. He had been in very tight spots before and had dexterously managed to wriggle through to live and thrive in another iteration. "Consultants can't help me at all," he told me several times.

Bill had consistently carried the day using his folksy Cajun charm, quick wit, indefatigable loquaciousness, determination, and entrepreneurial wiles. He was legendary in this way. Bill was among the most compelling salespeople I had ever met. Bill truly believed that Amedisys would not only pull through again and prosper, but that it would dominate the home care industry.

As good consultants, the BCG team and I wanted to get as much solid information as possible from our interactions with Bill. Accordingly, we parked ourselves near his office, in the small conference room I mentioned earlier. We had frequent meetings with him, generally at the end of the day. Bill was a hard worker and often cruised the building at night wanting to talk. We were happy to oblige him.

He would invite us into the boardroom and tell us what he was thinking. These were long, confusing affairs. They would stretch on for hours. He would launch into long monologues without displaying any interest in our take on things. His vision for the company and the industry were set in stone. Our analysis didn't matter much to him, so he largely ignored it. He also ignored our questions and guidance. During these late-night confabs, Bill would keep repeating his vision for the company. It was almost as if he believed the constant recitations of his vision could make it come true.

Although I started my career as a management consultant, it was never my passion. I did not like going back into consulting but felt obligated to David and admired Bill even though he wasn't listening to us. At the same time, I knew he and most other board members really wanted to understand what was going on inside the company specifically and, more broadly, where the industry was headed. Not knowing what else to do, I persevered, tolerated Bill's late-night ramblings, and dug even deeper into Amedisys's operations and strategies.

Several years prior when I was running strategy for the large health insurer Humana, we acquired a small home health company called Senior Bridge. Senior Bridge's services became transformative for many of Humana's Medicare enrollees. These members universally wanted to stay in their own homes. Senior Bridge helped them to do exactly that. It was particularly effective for members with complex medical conditions. I was convinced that care in the home was the key to taking better care of seniors and driving down their overall costs of care. My Senior Bridge experience and my belief in its business model infused our recommendations to the Amedisys board.

My hope was to deliver our work to the Amedisys board and move on. I had recently left Humana and was launching an innovative California-based company that took care of really sick Medicare enrollees with multiple chronic conditions. Our business model had three components: Build clinics in the neighborhoods where they lived, construct a huge database to track members and predict their needs, and have an insurance component that would put our money where our mouths were. It was new and exciting and very much where I felt healthcare's future was headed.

In contrast, I believed Amedisys was in its death throes with a defensive CEO advocating for a vision with no grounding in market realities. I felt Bill would take the good work that we had designed with his best people and shelve it. Toss it in the dumpster and never think about our analysis again.

As we were completing our work, I had a one-on-one session with Bill. He assured me that we had wasted his time and the company's resources. He said he would continue down the path he knew was right, despite our recommendations, despite the board, despite what the market was saying. It was going to be his way or the highway. He knew the home care business. We were just out-of-town interlopers.

Bill's vision was to build technology solutions that the whole industry would want once Amedisys demonstrated its prowess.

Amedisys would leverage its core home health business largely as a funding source and showcase for the company's technology. This would put Amedisys at the controlling nexus of the home care industry. Technology was the solution to driving better care, achieving more efficiencies, and delivering better profits. The company's monetization of the industry's dominant technology solution would move Amedisys away from the crowded and commoditized services it provided at the bottom of the healthcare food chain. This wasn't an unreasonable strategy, but it was far beyond Amedisys's zone of expertise.

After four months of work, the board asked us to present our final conclusions in a meeting at the Windsor Court Hotel in New Orleans. Jon Kaplan, BCG's lead healthcare director, and I made a joint presentation. We advocated that Amedisys return to its core home care businesses and find ways to differentiate the company's services by focusing on quality. Bill vociferously disagreed with most of our conclusions. Not surprisingly, he insisted that the strategy of building an industry-leading software platform was the key to Amedisys's long-term success.

In the midst of this corporate soul-searching, Amedisys was in trouble with the US government. The company generates almost all its revenue by delivering home health and hospice services to Medicare, Medicare Advantage, and Medicaid recipients. In one way or another, the US government funds over 95 percent of Amedisys's total business. The *Wall Street Journal* interviewed Amedisys and several other home care companies. The resulting article detailed the industry's aggressive sales practices and highlighted the lavish trips and bonuses that incentivized sales reps.

As a result of this article, the Department of Justice began investigating the sales practices of the nation's leading home healthcare providers. Amedisys was at the forefront of the DOJ's inquiries. The government reached relatively quick settlements with several of the leading home health players, but not Amedisys.

Instead of settling, Bill decided to fight the allegations and the government—the folks who made the rules and funded 95 percent of the company's revenues. By his actions, Bill defied the adage, "Never bite the hand that feeds you." It was a risky choice. Unlike the old Sonny Curtis and the Crickets song, "I Fought the Law and the Law Won," Bill had always beaten the odds by doing what he believed was right. So why not here?

In April 2014, Amedisys finally cried "Uncle." The company agreed to pay the government a $150 million penalty for its inappropriate billing practices. This amount was multiples higher than the fines the company's competitors had paid. Unlike Amedisys, they admitted responsibility early in the government's investigation and settled their disputes on much more favorable terms. The Amedisys resolution came with a corporate integrity agreement (CIA) that placed the company under probation for five years. During this period, Health and Human Services' Office of the Inspector General monitored the company's operations. The agreement also required Amedisys to report regularly on its compliance with Medicare's rules and regulations. Five years in the penalty box, $150 million in the hole, and a government watchdog hanging over the company's head.

After Jon and I finished with our final board presentation, there was a prolonged and contemplative silence. We had suggested an urgent and significant change of course for the company. We believed that Amedisys was on the wrong path. We were confident the company would fail if it continued on its present course.

Bill then vigorously argued against our ideas and suggested alternative routes to get to the promised land. His arguments though were not specifically against our particular issues or strategies. It was clear he had not carefully read the deck or had any intention of doing so. Our recommendations were irrelevant to him. He'd dumpster our work as quickly as he could and spray down the conference room we'd occupied, eliminating all trace of us. Bill's passion was admirable even though his conclusions were the opposite of ours and did not address the board's serious concerns regarding the company's long-term viability.

Bill was pleading with his handpicked board, of which he was the chairman, to trust him one more time. He'd done it before, and he'd do it again. But his tone was shrill. The down-home Cajun confidence was gone. The convincing colloquialisms and idioms weren't working. It was a sad moment.

David Pitts, our board sponsor who had fought Bill's active attempts to kill our engagement, asked us to leave and wait outside. We did. The anteroom chairs were uncomfortable. Obviously in the loop, the once-charming CEO's assistant at the desk outside the boardroom snarled at us. After an hour or so, David popped his head out of the boardroom and asked us to come back inside.

Bill was gone. It was a very quick meeting with one question. David asked us again if we believed the company was on the right track and if Bill could lead it out of the current mess. Jon deferred to me to answer. I responded, "I'm really sorry to say this, but I believe the company is heading into a wall and Bill is driving straight into it. He's drinking his own bathwater, and no one is telling him it's dirty." Pitts smiled, shook his head, and said that got the point across.

When I landed back home, David called me and said Bill had resigned. Would I be interested in the CEO role? He thought I would be good for it. I said, probably not. I doubted he could get the board behind me. The board and the company's employees would equate me with Bill's ouster. I then said to David: "People will look for the assassin of the charismatic leader. They'll turn to me and BCG. Blame me, blame the assassin even though Bill sowed the seeds of his own demise and pushing him out was your guys' decision."

I felt BCG and I had done our job well. We told them what we saw and what we felt was the truth. Our report was comprehensive. We worked in concert with the Amedisys executives running the business and developed market-driven solutions. We outlined a very promising path forward that the company's line leaders, who really knew the business, wanted implemented.

"Send me on my way," I said to David. "Bury us with the king. Look for untarnished leaders free of scars from the uprising. It's cleaner that way and gives everyone a fresh start. As you know, we didn't cause Bill's departure. He forced the issue himself. He did it to himself. But he's got a lot of loyal people in the company who will blame our work, not the fact that Bill was forcing the company down an impossible path. It's a pity. Bill is such a talented guy. I'm sorry we ended up opposing one another."

Months passed and nothing happened. I heard snippets and rumors of various people the board was trying to recruit for the CEO job as well as the fact the board was actively looking to solve the company's problems by selling it or merging it into a better-managed competitor.

I had moved on and was busy working to fund, build, and launch the complex care company in California. I was thoroughly engaged, striving to get this unique care model into the marketplace. Early reviews were very positive. We had a great, experienced team. We had one of the best private equity firms funding us. We even purchased a small chassis of a business to get us started. It was exciting! This was the future. Life was good.

Several months later, the company finally came back to me and asked me to become CEO. The Amedisys board had failed to merge or sell the company, and none of their preferred CEO candidates had accepted the job. I was the last, best, and only viable CEO candidate standing. I estimated that I had the enthusiastic support of only two out of the board's seven members. Another two reluctantly supported my selection. Not a dominant mandate for sure.

A headhunter's brutal honesty about my career prospects is what led me to accept the Amedisys CEO job and head to Baton Rouge. Ed Mullen, a senior healthcare partner at the prestigious executive search firm Korn Ferry, led the search to find Amedisys's next CEO. While the future of the California startup was promising, Ed reminded me that I was not the CEO. I was the president. The CEO was a very dominant and clear-visioned leader. With a healthy sense of the company's mission, he wanted things his way. The team's collective efforts were very much pieces and contributions to his dominant and singular vision of "his" company.

My question to Ed Mullen was pretty simple. "If I turn this job down, will I ever get a crack at being a CEO someday?" We were finishing up a lunch conversation under a palm tree in the parking lot of Ed's club in Santa Barbara, California. Ed thought a while, looked down, and then said with real sincerity, "No, I really doubt it." He continued, "This job isn't a picnic. I mean, you've looked under the hood. You know the challenges. If it were a great job, it would be filled by now. The chances are, this thing can't be turned around, so it's a big risk, and established people don't do big risks if they don't have to. If you want to get into the CEO club at this point in your career, you'll have to accept a dirty job that others won't."

My only reaction at this point in our conversation was to remember an interview I had with a Louisiana home health nurse when I was consulting with Amedisys. I had asked her what the company should do. It was "pretty simple," she said. "We take care of the patients, and you take care of us. We need someone to take care of us. You take care of us, and we'll pass it on to our patients, and then the company will be able to take care of itself."

And there it was, the Golden Rule, or at least a very clear virtuous circle. I had always wanted to apply my academic training in religion and philosophy to business. I had never intended to go into business and still had no idea how or why I got to where I was. But as I progressed in my career and veered toward healthcare, I began to see a way where my moral and philosophical beliefs could become ingrained within a business's DNA. Like seeds blowing through a desert, this seemed like a piece of fertile ground where my ideas and convictions could land and blossom.

A good business builds products and services that people need and want. Serving the needs of your customers and giving them the best you have is exactly equivalent to "treating someone the way you yourself want to be treated." Using the Golden Rule in healthcare amplifies the need for empathy and compassion. The people who receive care from Amedisys are very vulnerable, homebound, chronically sick, and frequently immobile, often suffering from multiple comorbidities. And in the case of hospice, actively dying. Amedisys's best people take it up a notch. They treat every patient as you would want your mom treated. It's their mantra.

If not taking direct care of patients, as many of Amedisys's employees don't (myself included), then it's their duty to help and enable the caregivers who do to be their best selves. Treat your front-line coworkers as you would your mom or as you yourself would want to be treated. When caregivers see Mom or Grandma in every face, compassion and extraordinary care follow. Great care requires compassion. The word *compassion* comes from the Latin *compati*, which means "to suffer with." To extend yourself into others' struggling situations and find a place to meet them. This made sense from all the work I did in my theology studies. In many religions, enlightenment is when you realize there is no "other"; everything has God in it. Compassionate care can lead you to this place.

I wear a cheap tin bracelet, pieced back together several times, that a Buddhist monk gave me when I was trekking in the Himalayas in Bhutan. It says in Sanskrit, "Om Mani Padme Hum," which translates into, "The Jewel Is in the Lotus." This is the "Om" the monks often chant over and over. The meaning of the Lotus mantra is that God is in everything. The lotus is a common flower, very beautiful, but it often grows out of muddy places and dunghills. The saying's meaning is simple and powerful—if you look into something that is beautifully common but has its roots in the mud and yet still see it as a jewel, your eyes and heart are opening to the godliness in everything around you in the same way that the lotus flower opens toward the sun.

This is how I translate that saying into the practice of healthcare: "God is everywhere; everyone is your mom!" The "mom" or "dad" in front of caregivers is someone's parent. When a caregiver treats a person with the depth and compassion with which they would treat their own parents, they honor that patient's godliness. Their acts spread compassionate caring into the broader world where it can multiply. Compassionate care creates wonderful interpersonal connections. Watching caregivers cross that bridge of compassion every day with their patients is truly inspirational. Namaste!

Amedisys clinicians and aides are in someone's home over 65,000 times a day. Our patients are at their most vulnerable. They have just left a hospital, nursing home, rehabilitation center, or assisted living facility. They are either recovering from surgery or have declined to the point where their physicians have determined they need care inside their home. If they are one of our hospice patients, they expect to die within three to six months.

When you strip it all down, most people are really good, admirable, and heroic in the face of pain, suffering, uncertainty, and oncoming death. Brave people at their best, facing the unadorned essentials of life and death.

Amedisys's best caregivers are truly miraculous in that they cross thresholds into unknown territory—someone else's home—and put their faith to work applying the Golden Rule in unfamiliar and, in some cases, unreceptive circumstances as best they can. Witnessing great caregiving is almost a religious experience: the empathy, the ritual of care, the focus, and, yes, unrequited compassion. In the best cases between a patient and the caregiver, that transference creates healing. If healing can't occur, transference generates acceptance and peace.

So that's why I took the job. I wanted to see if a business built around the Golden Rule could thrive and grow. To see if the ceaseless efforts to hire, train, and retain the best people to deliver that highest quality of care could reward our shareholders, the people who bet on us, with outsized economic returns. To show that healthcare economics could be deeply rooted in good intentions and moral behavior.

KEY TAKEAWAYS

- Most, if not all, experiences can be good ones if you learn from them and use that learning to benefit you in other ways. Much depends on how you frame learning experiences.
- Within all organizations are the seeds for extraordinary outcomes, both good and bad. The leader's job is to find the great seeds and cultivate and coax them forward.
- Sun Tzu, author of the often-quoted *Art of War*, was right. "If you know the enemy and if you know yourself, you need not fear the results of a hundred battles." Understanding who you are and what you are built for puts you in the right places to thrive. Being the right person in the right place will enable you to win more than half your battles. Position yourself where you know you are meant to be.
- If you really understand the market and constantly learn from it, you will never find yourself surprised or off course. Constantly learn from the people who make and deliver your products and services, as well as the customers who buy them.
- Your work is a manifestation of who you are. At its best, it will transform you as you transform what you are working on. Pick your jobs and assignments carefully.
- Embrace challenges. Go where others won't. Not recklessly but with full awareness that the incredible rewards that come from such stretching will far outweigh anything the paths of conformity and safety can bring. Unusual choices, "the road(s) less traveled," often turn out to be the most rewarding ones.
- If you are given a chance to lead, take it. Leadership is exhilarating and transformative.

- Find threads in your company's DNA that inspire you and your people. If you can make one of those threads a moral imperative, jump on it. Then weave a narrative around your imperatives. Make it a story that everyone wants to be a part of.
- Find ways for all your stakeholders to be a part of the company's story. Let them all in. If you can make them feel heroic, so much the better. Everyone wants and deserves the opportunity to become a hero.
- Find the good of what you do in your work life. As a leader, find and connect that good for all your employees. It gives them a higher purpose, and this will drive incredible energy and results.
- There is no "I" in company.

2

MY MEANDERING JOURNEY TO THE CORNER OFFICE

Right after I turned 14, my best friend's mom, Mrs. Farmer, pulled me out of my midmorning freshman math class. She and the school principal knocked on the door and then had a word with the teacher, who instructed me to go with them. They didn't say anything other than my friend's mom needed to take me home.

I grew up in rural Vermont and went to school in a unified school district. My high school served several small towns along the spine of the northern Green Mountains. I lived a long way from school. Mrs. Farmer and I knew each other well. Her three boys were soccer stars. At that time, two were playing in college, while her son Eddy and I were tearing it up in high school on a strong varsity team. The three of us had been on numerous long rides together for soccer games all over the state.

Normally we joked around and chatted. It was a crisp and beautiful October day. The regular soccer season was concluding. The state championships were about to begin. At that stage in my life, nothing was more important to me. Eddy and I liked to banter about the obnoxious coach who made us crawl up the grass hill behind the soccer field "like the pond slime you are" on our stomachs after a bad practice or losing a game. These were not the times where everyone got a juice box and a trophy. This trip with just Mrs. Farmer and me was eerily quiet. Something seemed wrong.

My family lived on an old hill farm at the foot of the state's largest mountain. Our house was at the end of a long dirt road lined with huge ancient sugar maple trees. On that day, the trees' leaves were a brilliant orange.

When we came up the hill to our white New England farmhouse, I saw my younger brother sitting and weeping on the stone doorstep. My mom, covered in bandages, came running to the car. Our pastor was right behind her. Still in the car, I looked at Mrs. Farmer and said, "Please don't make me get out." She was crying now and replied, "You have to. You have no choice."

My father was a very fine man. He was our town's doctor and a professor at the University of Vermont Medical School in Burlington, Vermont's biggest city. At that moment, he was lying unconscious in the hospital after a big-rig truck crushed his small VW Beetle. My mother and father were driving in separate cars to Burlington. My father's car had been stalling out, and they were taking it to a mechanic for repairs. The car started to sputter, so he pulled over. My mom pulled up ahead of him. Moments later, the truck smashed into Dad's car, which careened into Mom's car. The impact threw Mom into a nearby meadow. She sustained minor injuries. My dad was crushed inside the car, fighting for his life. The truck driver had fallen asleep, left the road, and hit the two small cars.

Dad took over two months to die. Those remaining at home struggled. Our family consisted of me, my parents, my younger brother, Karl, and my younger sister, Adrie. Mom went to the hospital every day trying to will my dad back to consciousness. On some days there were slivers of hope, flutters of his eyes, but when he finally died, there was nothing left of him. He was just a crushed skeleton of a man.

My mom did not want us to see him. One day in late November, I skipped school, hitchhiked into town, and snuck into the hospital through a loading-dock tunnel. I found my dad's room and peered at him from the hall. With one look, I knew the answer. My mom couldn't see straight. She had been clinging to false hopes. Dad was gone and wasn't coming back. I hitchhiked home, walked the last five miles off the main road home, through the farmland on the flats, through our village past the church and general store, and up the dirt road to our farm in the hills. I had no idea what Dad's death would mean for our family.

The year that followed was even worse than the time waiting for Dad to die. My mom went into deep mourning and became almost catatonic. We had no money. She started working to make ends meet, but her zombie-like behavior and commitment to her grieving kids meant jobs didn't last.

Nature has no sympathy; you either move forward or become prey. Nature abhors and then fills a void. Predators emerge to exploit vulnerability and weakness. The good folks of our little town banded together and looked after us, but jackal-like creeps watched and waited to take advantage. My mother held things together as best she could, but she was deeply in love with my father and couldn't countenance his violent end. We all had a hard time functioning. For a good six months, the four of us wandered around punch-drunk with grief.

Into this maelstrom, some deeply flawed and disturbed people started to appear. They were good at ingratiating themselves into our lives. For a brief while, my family intermingled with disturbed people.

We didn't have the strength to resist them. There is no greater fear than being defenseless against people you fear. When that happened, men—and they were all men—slapped and punched me. They challenged me to try to do something about it. They looked at my little sister and licked their lips. They forced me to shoot pistols and rifles with them near my house. If I refused, they threatened to shoot me. Amid the immense grief and our collective vulnerability, life became very scary.

It was brutally cruel and deeply unfair to go through this ordeal as a 14-year-old boy, but the experience did toughen me up and enlighten me. I entered a different world. With the hard-learned knowledge foisted upon me, I saw possibilities and angles on life I never could have imagined before my father's tragic death. Possibilities and probabilities I never would have considered became part of my thought process and, paradoxically, enabled me to develop a richer and more textured understanding of life's vicissitudes. Life could be unfair; everything you had could change completely in a moment; people behaved differently under tough circumstances.

Despite the chaos or perhaps because of it, I experienced moments of extreme clarity during this time of extreme imbalance. I have come to believe these glimpses were an extraordinary gift borne of an excruciating experience. Our family had been torn apart. I knew what I had to do to rebuild my life. No one was going to bail me out. I got it. I had to go out on my own. Let Mom remarry, which she did, and take care of my sister. At age 14, it was time for me to leave home behind.

I had no central role in our family dynamics anymore. Hanging around would not help anyone. "Things fall apart; the center cannot hold/Mere anarchy is loosed upon the world" and "The ceremony of innocence is drowned," as the poet Yeats famously wrote in "The Second Coming." I applied to a small boarding school in southern Vermont and got a full scholarship. I lasted a semester. Only 15, I left school to travel through Europe. When I returned to the states, I worked as an assistant tennis pro and racquet stringer in Cape Cod. I slept on a cot in the pro's boathouse, listening to the ocean tides splashing against the pilings.

Underneath it all, I knew that education was the ticket to the good life in America. That had been my dad's route. He was the son of German immigrants who had followed a well-worn path to work at General Electric in Schenectady, New York. My dad's father was a very skilled machinist and lathe operator. He designed and built complex parts for GE engines.

His son, my dad Bert, went to nearby Union College. Union was and is a very good school. My dad was both an academic and a tennis star there. When World War II intervened, he enlisted and commanded a small minesweeper in the Aleutian Islands northeast of Japan. When the war ended, he enrolled at Yale Medical School under the GI Bill. While there, he designed and built a working artificial heart with his father's lathe. It kept a large dog alive for several hours. With great career prospects, he left Yale to take a position in Vermont where he could teach medicine and continue his research on artificial hearts. My future mother also was in graduate school at Yale during this time. They met and married. After his war experience of fishing the bodies of Japanese kamikaze pilots from the ocean, he wanted to live in the countryside, raise his family on a farm, and and create a buffer between us and the chaos of the modern world. Sadly, this dream eluded him.

Before my father died, I was largely an indifferent student. I excelled at athletics and found comfort wandering through Vermont's woods. That's where I directed my time, passion, and effort. After my father's death, I realized that education was a must-win blood sport.

My world was chaos after Dad's death. In order not to go totally adrift, I tried to quickly establish little islands of stability, sanctuary, and validation—places where I could participate, get a stable foothold, have a couple of wins, and find security and safety. I gravitated toward safer, more controllable harbors. My passion for and success in school and athletics helped push the chaos away. The ground underneath me became more and more solid.

My siblings also believed that academic achievement could lead to a better, more stable life. Our mother and father were great examples and role models. Both were Yale-educated. They had achieved much by building up strong academic pedigrees.

My younger brother, Karl, discovered that the dean of Saint Paul's School, one of the nation's finest boarding schools, had a summer house on the side of our mountain. He biked five miles and walked up the last mile of dirt road to her house. With complete naivete, he told her he wanted to attend St. Paul's. It worked. Karl became a scholarship student, went to Wesleyan with me, and earned a PhD in art history from Yale, where he was a Mellon and Luce Fellow.

Karl is now the curator of the Princeton University Museum. He has an endowed chair from the university. He teaches at Princeton and is the author and editor of several prize-winning books on society's changing attitudes, as depicted in the arts, regarding power and the environment.

My little sister, Adrie, was nine years old when our father died. In many ways, she suffered the most of the three kids. She went with my mother to Seattle, got into the posh Lakeside School (Bill Gates's alma mater), went to Amherst College graduating as a Phi Beta Kappa, and got her PhD in anthropology at Harvard. Adrie is now an award-winning professor, author, published poet, and philanthropist. Her philanthropy builds schools for young girls in Sudan.

While I was on Cape Cod, I followed my brother's daring example and rode my bike 15 miles in a borrowed suit to the summer home of Deerfield Academy's director of admissions. Deerfield was one of

the jockier boarding schools in the country. He was stunned and baf-
flingly impressed at the sweaty mess on his doorstep who was request-
ing admission to his school. As I reached into my satchel to hand him
a wrapped parcel of my best schoolwork along with an essay about
why I wanted to go to Deerfield, his wife invited me into their home.
The three of us sat at a table while I tried to explain why I needed to go
to Deerfield. She teared up when I said, "I just need a place to go to for
a little while." He let me in as a junior transfer despite my lack of academic accomplishment. I'm sure his wife helped my cause.

Moving to a top-tier boarding school as a junior from a rural
Vermont high school was probably not the best idea. I was completely unprepared. At my high school in Vermont, I was at the
top of my class with just a couple hours of homework each day. At
Deerfield, the work required triple that effort plus weekends. The
school's advanced curriculum was beyond me. Despite heroic efforts,
I couldn't leapfrog into an accomplished student overnight. Instead,
I simply outworked and outcharmed everyone else. At the end of my
junior year I was third from the last in my class. At the end of my
senior year, I was third from the top.

My disastrous academic performance during my junior year
limited my college choices. I took a flyer on Wesleyan University, a
"Little Ivy" school in Middleton, Connecticut. Their soccer coach
had expressed interest. Much to my surprise, Wesleyan admitted me.
My college advisor told me I'd beaten the odds and gotten into a
much better school than he'd expected. Just to make sure, I called the
school's director of admissions to confirm my admission. He assured
me I was exactly what Wesleyan wanted: "Someone who still had a lot
to prove." I was determined to make sure the admissions people never
regretted their decision.

Two years at Deerfield had gotten me on par with the privileged
kids from the fancy schools and elite backgrounds. When I arrived at

Wesleyan, I was well prepared, knew how to study, and was still smoldering with shame from my poor academic record during my junior year at Deerfield. I did have something to prove.

I attacked college life with a vengeance. While I played varsity soccer and squash with a year of tennis, my real accomplishments occurred off the playing fields. I was elected to Phi Beta Kappa, won four academic prizes, was editor in chief of the college newspaper, and chaired the college Judiciary Board. Best of all, I met my future wife, Serena, at Wesleyan.

During my senior year, the Rhodes Trust awarded me a three-year scholarship to attend Oxford University in the United Kingdom. This scholarship covered full tuition and provided stipends for study and travel. I had become a Rhodes Scholar. No one, particularly me, could have predicted that achievement from my 15-year-old self. Even though I missed my dad enormously, his death and its aftermath triggered my ambition to get the most out of life as it did for Karl and Adrie.

Even Mom went back to school. She earned a PhD at age 60 and became a college professor. After several one-year appointments at second-tier colleges in Florida, Oregon, West Virginia, and Boston, Mom joined the faculty at the University of Vermont where my dad had been a professor. Talk about coming full circle. At age 64, she won a coveted Fulbright Fellowship and moved to Zimbabwe to teach and do research at the University at Harare. We are all so proud of her. She is the toughest of us all.

My family's academic achievements raise an interesting question. Are we stratospherically smart or cut from different cloth than other people? Absolutely not! Dad's sudden and horrific death spurred us individually and collectively to get the most out of life. For a brief period, we got an unvarnished glimpse of how unforgiving the world could be. In response, we got serious. We knew we had to give it all we had to reach safer ground.

Grit by Angela Duckworth chronicles how success in school or work results primarily from having the ability to pursue goals despite obstacles and setbacks. This "can-do" concept is quintessentially American. Enduring, learning from, and refusing to succumb to failure is a part of grit. It builds character and resilience, teaches lessons, and sets the stage for subsequent success.

The questions that particularly interest me focus on how people become gritty. What lights the fire? What's the catalyst? Are you born with grit? Are all people born with it, and they just need to find it? Or is there a switch someplace that ignites grit? Or is it some combination of all these things?

In discussing the potential origins of grit, Duckworth provides an interesting insight into how extreme adversity or trauma can trigger positive personal development. She cites research by two famous psychologists, Steven Maier and Martin Seligman. They developed an experiment for two groups of adolescent rats. The experiment subjected both groups of rats to electric shocks. The first group could stop the shocks by moving a wheel in their cage. By doing so, they could alleviate their pain. The second group did not have that option. They had no recourse against the shocks. These two groups of rats exhibited very different behaviors in adulthood. The rats who could control the shocks were more adventurous and confident. The ones who couldn't were more timid and insecure.

Duckworth interviewed Maier on what she termed the "neurobiology of hope." Maier responded as follows:

> If you experience adversity that you overcome on your own during your youth, you develop a different way of dealing with adversity later on. It's important that the adversity be

pretty potent because the brain areas really have to rewire together in some new fashion. That just doesn't happen with just minor inconveniences.

Maier subsequently explained that brain circuitry, particularly in younger people, can rewire itself to respond more effectively to lightning bolts of stress. With rewired brain circuitry (sometimes termed "neuroplasticity"), these people say and believe, "I can do something about this," when confronting adversity. Constructive action follows this thought.

Conversely, according to Maier, humans exposed to ongoing stress get beaten down and decline into defeated timidity. Seligman and Maier term this the "learned helplessness" syndrome. Friedrich Nietzsche's famous observation, "That which does not kill us, makes us stronger," can apply. Resilience has its origins in overcoming adversity. The key word is "overcoming." Unrelenting punishment without the ability to do anything about it can crush individuals and eviscerate their resilience.

In 1959, a popular Yale literature professor named Richard Sewall published *The Vision of Tragedy*. Sewall's book ties the great tragedies of Shakespeare, Sophocles, and Aeschylus to the philosophies of Aristotle, Nietzsche, and Schopenhauer. In their unique ways, these playwrights and philosophers explored the concept of what Sewall termed "tragic vision." Plato's idea of "the shadows and forms" embodies this concept. Humans cannot see and face truth directly. They can only see it obliquely, as Plato famously describes, "like watching shadows on a cave wall." Tragic vision describes the brief moments of extreme clarity of vision and thought that individuals experience in response to adversity. These moments can be life-altering.

Expanding on this theme, Sewall paraphrases Nietzsche by concluding that tragedy is the noblest of existences. At the apex of their tragic revelations with their false perceptions stripped away, heroes like Oedipus and King Lear develop a brutally clear worldview. They see things as they really are, not how they want them to be. Sewall argues that tragic events reveal the truth behind the veil. As people's self-constructed worlds evaporate, they glimpse essential truths. The reward for their suffering is a clear glimpse of truth about the world and themselves. In this way, tragic vision gives them the power to understand and address elemental forces.

Pretty grim, but developing Sewall's type of tragic vision at age 14 altered the course of my life. While I would not want to relive the heart-rending experiences of my youth, they shocked my system of thinking, rewired my brain, and forced me to develop true grit. Those capabilities have made all the difference. There are good and bad cycles in life. Really bad experiences can rock an individual to their core, but they also can trigger wisdom, clarity, and unexpected strength. By overcoming tragedy, many not only endure but rise, phoenix-like, from the ashes to achieve unanticipated joy and success in their lives.

KEY TAKEAWAYS

- The experience of living through my father's death and its consequences is what molded me into the individual I am today.
- Humans are hardwired to rebound from adversity and gain valuable, hard-earned knowledge in the process. Never experiencing hard times means having limited self-knowledge and capacity to respond constructively when hard times do present themselves, which they undoubtedly will.
- The glass is always half full. With this positive attitude, individuals can transform personal difficulties and suffering into useful knowledge for leading a happy and productive life. To paraphrase the Buddha, "No experience is a bad one."
- Grit, the ability to take hits and keep coming back, is an essential quality for people and organizations in our ever-changing and hard-to-predict world. People become resilient and function at their fullest potential when they have the grit and its associated internal properties to weather tough times.
- The clarity of vision that emerges from a testing or traumatic period is a gift. Use it and remember its lessons. Hard-won knowledge is the most valuable and enduring but also the most exacting.
- Humans cannot perpetually live in the extreme. It's too hard. Come down from the mountaintop and remember the lessons and clarity from your trials. By assimilating them, you will make the rest of your life much more enjoyable.

3

WALKABOUT (HOW THE EMPEROR GOT NEW CLOTHES)

The first thing I needed to do when I arrived at Amedisys in December 2014 was learn the company's strategy and determine if and how it should change. During my time consulting with Amedisys, I had concluded that the company's strategy of becoming an industrywide technology provider was off track, but I needed to make sure.

After my initial conversations with the leaders of our company's new technology platform, AMS3, I questioned whether my first impression of our technology strategy was wrong. Everyone at corporate headquarters emphasized to me how powerful and transformative our technology could become. I reviewed detailed workflow architecture and schemas, heard the chorus of attributes the technology would offer, and began to warm to the idea that this new technology platform could be transformative. I began to get excited and thought, "This Amedisys gig might be easy." It might be a "twofer" (a two-for-one deal) where all I would have to do is fund development of the technology platform and watch Amedisys migrate from a commodified, out-of-favor services provider into a differentiated tech-enabled solutions company for the entire home care industry. The magic would occur organically.

The team was testing the new AMS3 technology at several care centers in the field. The reported results were very positive. Since I felt that I was one of the luckiest people in the world having landed on such a transformative technology, I wanted to see the platform in action for myself. So I got in the car and traveled to the three sites in Louisiana where the technology was getting its test run.

It turned out that the benefits of the new technology platform were entirely in the idealistic eyes of its creators and corporate proponents. At the first test site, the care center's staff almost jumped across the table as they started yelling at me, "What the f**k are you doing to us!" The second care center was more subdued, but equally dissatisfied. Several people cried, which in many ways was worse. Their shoulders drooped, their heads went down, and the tears flowed. The third visit was not a Goldilocks moment where the porridge was just right. Just the opposite. The staff stared at me in stony silence and refused to speak. Their collective hostility was palpable.

Appropriately sensitized, I then arranged patient visits with nurses to see how they used the technology. I knew how to do basic workflow mapping and wanted to understand how frontline caregivers applied the technology. I needed to know whether the platform was salvageable. Perhaps we just needed better training. At first, the technology platform seemed to perform well; then I realized the futility of running new age tech on old computers. It was a nightmare.

Care documentation, necessary for follow-up care and billing, could not be done on-site in the patient's home. This system flaw created more work for frontline nurses and therapists. They had to compile care notes in the field and then subsequently enter relevant data (in the office or at home) into their old, outdated computers. Our billing procedures required same-day submission of care notes. Most clinicians were working late into the night to complete their visit notes in a timely fashion. Needless to say, clinicians who spend their evenings documenting care notes didn't appreciate the cumbersome and duplicative work. Life's too short. Many began looking for jobs elsewhere. Corporate's insistence on using the new technology platform was making the work lives of our frontline caregivers miserable, which was creating its own set of problems. They were leaving Amedisys in droves.

The info that corporate staff were feeding me regarding our tech platform was completely wrong. This technology wasn't our salvation. It was actually harmful. No other home care companies would ever use it. Moreover, our continued use of AMS3 would drive even more of our people out the door. AMS3 was creating an enormous HR problem.

As my support for the technology platform wavered, its proponents went into high gear defending it. Now the people jumping across the desk and yelling at me were the corporate people in charge of this "transformational technology." We had spent $70+ million and were continuing to invest millions each year in development. The project's design and support staff exceeded 200 people, approximately 40 percent of our corporate workforce. We were betting the farm on this potential white elephant. I needed to do something, fast.

I brought in one of my most trusted advisors to look under the hood. Ralph Judah is a spicy, blunt, super-smart South African management consultant. The South African government first imprisoned and then expelled Ralph for organizing against apartheid. My semi-humorous advice to my Amedisys colleagues working with him was cautionary: "Don't cross Ralph. From prison, he knows how to shank people." He was a loyal and tough hombre.

Ralph has a preternatural ability to get to the essence of problems quickly. Unlike most consultants, Ralph never sugarcoats the truth. That's why I love him. He quickly got to the brutal truth regarding AMS3, and he had his own tech consultant validate his intuition and delivered the following verdict: "You must kill AMS3, or it will kill the company. Kill it now because you don't have much time. This project is sucking the life out of an already teetering company."

The company was bleeding cash it didn't have on this project, so I followed Ralph's advice. I killed AMS3 cold turkey and laid off most of the 200+ people involved in the project. I hate laying people off, so we made sure that anyone who wanted a job in another area of the company that was either hiring internally or expanding got one. Alternatively, we helped people land jobs externally. Our HR department worked hard to make sure all our laid-off professionals who needed a job found one.

People often judge an organization by how it treats them going out the door. There is nothing worse than being ignominiously tossed out of the workplace where you have devoted so much of your precious time and energy. I wanted to make sure that we treated the people who needed to leave the company well. I wanted them and the people who remained employed at Amedisys to believe that the company had acted honorably, that we had done our absolute best to help our former colleagues manage their transition. We sponsored and hosted job fairs where we invited outside companies to interview and vet our people. I also made several calls to local CEOs who were hiring to suggest they consider our people. We ultimately found new positions for almost all the laid-off professionals. I felt very good about this.

Over the years this effort, our collective effort to help our displaced colleagues, paid off in a myriad of ways. It enabled us to build a differentiated brand as an employer in our market. Yes, some people were angry that AMS3 was not going forward. Others got it, realized a fight was futile, and took advantage of our offers of help. Those who did receive help told their stories to anyone who would listen. Even though Amedisys was still struggling financially, our reputation as a company soared in the marketplace. It was evident that we cared about all our people even when we had to separate from them. That message played exceptionally well.

Ultimately, a company like ours is only as good as the people it employs. Treat them well, and they will treat customers well. This is the "loyalty effect" in action. My belief in the Golden Rule for managing our company was paying some early dividends.

When the company did turn around, we would need to rebuild and began hiring new employees. Prospective new hires were eager to talk with us. Even some former employees, who had left the company in frustration, returned and reengaged. They wanted to work at the "new company," now that it clearly acknowledged the importance of its people.

There is a finite amount of talent in every market. Those who work in specific industries gain an understanding of their competitors. When I arrived as CEO, Amedisys had an employee turnover rate greater than 40 percent. That meant Amedisys essentially turned over its entire workforce every two and a half years. Not everyone left, of course. Amedisys had many long-tenured employees, but the company was experiencing an exceptionally heavy and destructive churn. As we dug in, we discovered our turnover was concentrated in nursing, those responsible for Amedisys's ability to deliver great care. Not good.

For me, the high nursing turnover represented an opportunity to understand the day-to-day dynamics of our frontline caregivers. Particularly in small or medium-sized home care markets, most nurses either had worked for us at some point in their career or at least knew us by reputation. Most had probably at least interviewed with us. I had our team compile a list of Amedisys alumni, nurses who had once worked for us and left. I wanted to know why.

We conducted a small research project where we called these ex-employees/alumni and asked them if they would ever consider coming back to work at Amedisys. To my surprise and delight, over 75 percent said they would. Either they had had a good experience with us, or they had heard the company had changed. In either case, they were willing to give us another try. This provided a golden opportunity to test my Golden Rule managerial approach.

Several years ago, there was a brief article in the *Harvard Business Review* that chronicled the value of alumni. According to the article, hiring and onboarding alumni is easier and less costly than hiring new employees. Rehires are 40 percent more productive in their first quarter of work and stay longer on the job. That made me laser-focused on rehiring our alumni nurses to jump-start expansion of our frontline staff.

When I was at McKinsey, which in my opinion has the best corporate alumni program, only one of eleven entering consultants become directors and stay with the firm. That means ten of those eleven people, representing over 90 percent of McKinsey's consulting workforce, leave the company for alternative employment. This included me. I left McKinsey after two years with the firm. To its credit, McKinsey turns what could be a brutal negative experience (getting fired) into a positive one. It celebrates its employees when they leave, importantly recognizing their contributions to the firm. It doesn't stop there. McKinsey helps place its departing consultants in great new positions. It uses its powerful alumni network to optimize the probability of gainful new employment. Very few consultants walk out the McKinsey doors without knowing exactly what they're going to do next.

So when consultants left McKinsey, it was a positive experience. So what do McKinsey alumni do when they need to hire consultants? They call the firm that trained them and managed their transition to bigger opportunities. When they need to hire great people, they call McKinsey for advice and prospects. Beyond that, McKinsey cultivates its alumni network as a valuable source of market intelligence. Information flows both ways. Trusted relationships deepen. Everybody wins.

What McKinsey does again that is brilliant is celebrate its consultants for being part of its special club. Those consultants who don't make it all the way to director are remarkably talented and capable professionals. The fact that their alumni once wore the McKinsey jersey is a huge accomplishment. Their alumni continue to wear the McKinsey badge with honor long after they've left the firm. It's a brilliant twist on repositioning professionals not destined to make the firm's top tier. Once on the outside, the "rejected" alumni don't spurn their former employer. They do their best to help McKinsey grow and prosper. This occurs because McKinsey celebrates its alumni's time at the firm even as it's aggressively culling its herd. It occurs because McKinsey actively cultivates alumni relationships over the long term and it honors all its employees, even those who don't get to ring the director's bell.

McKinsey's approach to alumni management made enormous sense to me. Lessons learned. I was determined to replicate its approach in each of our markets. Amedisys's pool of potential caregivers is incredibly limited. It never pays to cut ties as employees leave. Let's elevate their experience, take care of them on the way out, make them a part of the Amedisys club, celebrate their time with us, keep getting better as a place to work, and keep in touch so when they want to come back, we're here—arms open waiting for them.

The results have been very encouraging. We made turnover a science and reduced it from over 40 percent down to 18 percent in a high-turnover industry. Turnover is both expensive and resource depleting. It takes time to train and acculturate new employees. Once on the job, it takes time and hands-on experience to deliver high-quality care. Reducing turnover enhances clinical care delivery, improves the productivity of our clinicians, and turbocharges margin growth. Reducing turnover generated exponential returns to our business. This isn't rocket science. People are roughly 85 percent of Amedisys's costs. Creating a work environment where employees want to stay and make a career is the key to providing great care and achieving great economics.

Alumni rule. During my tenure at Amedisys, we created an active alumni network that keeps our former employees in touch and up-to-date with the company. We constantly remind them of their connection and value to the company. In turn, there are many more "boomerangs," employees who leave and return, today than ever before. Alumni are the best source of new employees. They also are the best source for referrals. When both employees and alumni who want to return realize that Amedisys is the best place for them personally and professionally, they settle in, become one with the company, and stop looking for employment elsewhere.

Among my proudest accomplishments was having Amedisys named as one of the Best Places to Work by *Modern Healthcare*, the leading publication in the healthcare services industry. We worked for over five years to achieve this distinction and have made it for a second consecutive year in 2022. This acknowledgment is very important in the industry, where caregivers are often treated like commodities. More times than not, if a company makes that list, prospective employees will consider it for employment.

Amedisys's evolution, turnaround, and subsequent success have centered on people. My obvious but strong realization was that our people are everything. They are at least as smart and as informed as I am. Once I realized as CEO that everyone is on the same level, I worked tirelessly to find ways to unleash the tremendous human potential that was right in front of me.

In a decentralized, often hierarchical, industry, this can be hard to do, but it's also the right thing to do. Again the Golden Rule—treat people the way you yourself want to be treated—must be the governing principle. That means ferreting out unfairness, communicating as much as you can, listening as hard as you can, and walking the talk. Getting rid of the organizational "craw stickers," the inequitable practices that really bug and agitate your people, is essential. For me as CEO, that meant building a whole infrastructure of institutional listening within Amedisys. I strove to give our employees and patients an important voice. A consistent voice keeps a company's leaders both up-to-date and honest. When leaders stop listening hard every day, they often get in trouble.

When I started at Amedisys, the company had stopped listening for years. It was a loose confederacy of 300+ care centers in 34 states. My key objective for moving the company forward was enabling our care centers to market and operate autonomously while becoming culturally consistent by applying core Golden Rule values ubiquitously. To accomplish this, we needed to create a strong culture of encouraging all voices to speak, actively listening to their feedback, and then acting appropriately in response.

Getting the culture right was essential. We also had to find another technology solution to record our visits in accordance with clinical, regulatory, and billing requirements. It's important to keep accurate records to document workflows and ongoing patient status. It was quite clear that the AMS3 solution was not working and we needed to ween ourselves off that system. I hired some experts in home-based healthcare technology who once again verified that AMS3 was "vapor wear." They gave us an analysis of what the industry was using, what was working, and what wasn't.

At that point, I assembled a group of users and gave them the authority to select the company's technology platform. I could think of nothing worse than me making the decision and forcing it on the organization. What did I know about clinical workflow, nursing, or physical therapy, or about coding home health and hospice visits? People inside the company were smarter than I was on these subjects. Their work lives were dependent on whatever technology decisions the company made, so why not let them make and own the decision. I let go and trusted the process.

We brought in everyone who wanted to give input, reviewed all the options, got all the stakeholders in a room, and made our choice. And the winner was, drumroll please, Home Care Home Base (HCHB). HCHB was a software platform built by a competitor that worked much better than AMS3. It was a controversial decision. Many believed we should have our own in-house solution, but I believed the task force had made the right choice. More importantly, people who needed to use this software day in and day out had made the choice. By delegating the decision to the task force, the organization demonstrated it had enough depth and knowledge in-house to make a tough call. In the process, our employees became responsible stewards for the company's resources. They earned a seat at the table for directing the company's future.

The goodwill generated from this strategic move was astounding. Our people made sure their chosen technology worked. It was theirs now, not something management had foisted on them like AMS3. Employee ownership of major strategic decisions increases the chances of success exponentially. This was a good learning for me—trust your people, and they will make the right choices. My role was to facilitate the process so our people could make the best choices for the company.

I used this inclusive approach to making another major strategic decision regarding our corporate headquarters. As I said earlier, the building was a converted big-box grocery store, Schwegmann's. It was huge and cavernous. The core of the renovated building was open to encourage collaboration. Also, as mentioned earlier, my predecessor had taken part of the old building and created an isolated C-suite that required a special passkey for entry. Executives would often go for days without visiting the open workspaces where our corporate staff toiled away. One of the first things I did was move out of the executive offices into a glass conference room in the middle of the open space. None of the executives I inherited went with me. Needless to say, none of these folks remain with the company today.

After a flood hit Baton Rouge in 2016, it became apparent to me that our current location was a risky place to have our headquarters. Rising waters came close to flooding our servers. More importantly, the space itself was horrible. It was dark, echoey, and boxy. Great companies should have great places for their people to work, and we wanted to become a great company. With some help, I managed to find a buyer for our headquarters building at an extraordinarily good price, much higher than we expected. So we sold the building.

Many employees freaked out, thinking this was the first of several sly moves to exit Baton Rouge. We had opened an office in Nashville, the epicenter of the healthcare world, to attract the diverse and experienced talent we needed to transform the company. These types of professionals were not readily available in Baton Rouge. The Baton

Rouge people feared this was a veiled step toward migrating the company headquarters to Tennessee, like so many other healthcare companies had done.

Confronted with dissension in the ranks, I pulled out the same playbook I used to select the best software platform. I turned the decision regarding the corporate headquarters over to our folks. And what happened? They did great! We established an employee committee, then we visited various sites in Baton Rouge and selected the best location. We had a team of office-based employees design the new office layout.

It's easy to hate office space, but our people stepped up to the task of designing an aesthetically pleasing and functional working environment. Those not involved in the design process trusted their colleagues to make the right decisions. Once the renovation was completed and we moved in, everyone including me loved the new space. It is open, sunny, democratic, and collaborative. As it turns out, Amedisys didn't need a fancy architect to interpret our corporate office needs. Our people, with assistance of our real estate team, stepped in and got the job done. I'm very proud of the work they did and love spending time there.

Why do I work this way? It came from my "walkabout." For those of you not familiar with the term, a walkabout is a rite of passage for young male Aborigines in the Australian Outback. Still teenagers, these boys must survive in the wilderness alone for a fixed period of time, sometimes up to a year. The walkabout is an arduous spiritual and physical test. It fosters high levels of self-knowledge and self-awareness. Participants learn about themselves and their responsibilities to the tribe. Upon their return, these boys initiate into the tribe as men.

My walkabout was an intense initiation into Amedisys and the home care industry. A couple of months after I joined the company, I realized that I needed to know much more about Amedisys if I were to be an effective CEO, particularly since the advice I was receiving from the people at corporate headquarters was skewed and self-serving. It wasn't in sync with what the marketplace was demanding. I needed a new source of nourishment after the warm bathwater I'd been drinking. Their misinformation was not malicious. It was the by-product of strategic insights generated inside out from the corporate offices rather than outside in from the marketplace. Their advice, such as it was, reflected internal, not market-based, dynamics.

Overall, the company was also in much worse shape than I had thought. It was strategically aimless. The staff were demoralized. The company financials were horrible. Every day, surprises and new crises bludgeoned me. Fighting so many immediate fires, I found it hard to develop an appropriate perspective and plan longer term.

At this time I often reflected on this piece of advice given to me by a turnaround expert: "When there is still nasty incoming bombarding you and the stream of surprises creeping out from the closet of horribles hasn't lessened, you haven't hit bottom yet." I was desperate to find "terra firma" but quickly concluded that I would not find it inside company headquarters. So very quickly after I joined the company, I packed a suitcase and left for close to two months to visit our care centers. I figured nothing worse could happen, and if it did, headquarters had my number and could find me. Besides, I desperately needed to experience our frontline operations up close and personal.

I traveled to 17 states and visited over 34 care centers. My routine was to show up at a care center and say, "I'm the new guy in town.

What do I need to know? Tell me about what we do right, what we need to improve on, and what we need to fix that's ruining us." I went on patient visits with clinicians from most of the care centers into all sorts of settings. I listened to the hospitals, SNFs (skilled nursing facilities), IRFs (inpatient rehabilitation facilities), ALFs (assisted living facilities), ILFs (independent living facilities), and physician offices that sent business our way. I also talked to people who had chosen not to use Amedisys and their reasons for that decision. Many had strong feelings and weren't hesitant to share them. I listened and took copious notes at every encounter. After two months of conversations that filled several of my colorful notebooks, common themes and truths emerged. The collective chorus of opinions clarified and became stronger. I now believed I understood what we were trying to do, what the people who used our services wanted from us, what the market was clearly signaling, and where we could add value.

Most importantly, this trip left me very excited about Amedisys's future and the future of care in the home. I came back thinking, "We can do this! It's going to be great!"

On my walkabout, I presumed I knew nothing because I really didn't know anything. I was willfully ignorant of Amedisys, what we stood for, how the marketplace perceived us, and what we should be doing. My focus narrowed. I needed to know what our patients, employees, and referral sources thought of us. I craved a deep understanding of how our company was or was not responding to marketplace needs. Walking about the right way reveals all.

During my walkabout, I thought a lot about Socrates, the Greek philosopher made famous by his student Plato. In Plato's essay "The Apology," he chronicles Socrates's trial for the crime of corrupting the youth of Athens. Socrates was a self-defined "gadfly" to the state of Athens. He constantly questioned the basic tenets of Athenian society. Eventually the ruling authorities got sick of Socrates's incessant moral questioning. They arrested, tried, and found him guilty, and then they put him to death by making him drink hemlock.

"Apologia" means "defense" in Greek, so "The Apology" is Socrates's defense of himself. During his trial, Plato reported that Socrates was accused of claiming he was the world's wisest man. Socrates explained that when the famed Oracle at Delphi first made that declaration, he thought the presumption was absurd.

The Oracle at Delphi sat near a sacred spring on the side of Mount Parnassus, the center of the Greek world. It was Athens's highest religious authority where priestesses (the sybils) would deliver obscure messages from the god Apollo. Socrates thought that this label was preposterous because he was very famous for saying he knew nothing. As Socrates noted in his defense, "How could a man who claimed he knew nothing be told he was the wisest man in all of Athens, all of Greece!" There must be wiser men than he.

So he went and met and listened to all the other men in Greece who were considered knowledgeable and wise. After he had met and listened to all these wise men, he recanted and said he agreed with the Oracle's proclamation. Socrates came to that conclusion because he at least admitted he "knew nothing," whereas all the other supposedly wise men were full of their own opinions and biases. When examined, their renown opinions fell apart; their logic did not hold. As Plato captures in "The Apology," Socrates drove home the point with his famous observation that "the unexamined life is not worth living."

For Socrates, wisdom requires honest inquiry and the rigorous testing of preconceived ideas to see if they can withstand scrutiny. I'm no Socrates, but for me admitting and pleading ignorance has never been a problem. Clearly, I had formed some opinions about Amedisys from my consulting engagement, my own experiences in the healthcare marketplace, and the field interviews I had conducted.

I had some understanding of market trends and where the pockets of opportunities might lie, but these "opinions" were far from rock solid. My thin interpretations of Amedisys's reality required validation. Were they right or off base? I needed to go out and keep asking questions, Socrates-like, until common, solid, sensible themes emerged. Only through rigorous inquiry and openness to market feedback could Amedisys create its version of truth.

I had an overwhelming and sinking feeling that our corporate strategies neither emanated from nor reflected the company's essence. I believed that there was a marvelous core embedded within Amedisys but that it wasn't shining through. We needed to find, tightly grab hold of our core strengths and expound on them. Once discovered and broadcast, our marvelous core would give every single Amedisys employee a reason to jump out of bed, values to live by, and a mission to be proud of.

I found that going out into the markets without any presuppositions or assumptions was liberating. It enabled me to ask very basic questions about what the marketplace valued and whether Amedisys measured up. In this painstaking and deliberate way, I learned what we did and did not do well, along with what our frontline caregivers needed to perform their vital work at the highest levels.

The layers of accumulated assumptions and wisdom guiding Amedisys's corporate decision-making didn't hold up when examined in the markets I visited. Asking the following three very basic questions got me closer to the true character of our operations:

- What did the market (market = our patients and those people who send patients to us) need from Amedisys?
- How did we and our competition fulfill those needs?
- What did we as a company do well, and what did we do poorly?

The accumulated answers to these questions from those on the front lines gave me a good idea about what we needed to do as a company.

The best thing you can do when chaos reigns is to find a point of focus. That point of focus is a strategy. The articulation of strategic goals evolves into a series of choices and tasks required to achieve those goals. A good strategy means saying no more than saying yes. When the strategy is set, leaders don't have to hem and haw about choices or options because they know where the company needs to go and how to get there. Strategy is about making informed choices and targeting efforts. Great strategy is the result of thinking everything through so hard that most choices are easy because they are obvious. Great strategies have purity of definition and vision. They light a clear path to a brighter future.

The American poet Wallace Stevens wrote a funny little poem called the "Anecdote of the Jar." It's 12 short lines about someone placing a jar on a hill in Tennessee, and how everything falls around and orders itself around it. The act of putting a jar on a hill defines that world, creating a center with a focus and an order. Everything must now revolve around it.

To me, that's what strategy is. It's that jar or stake you pound into place that defines everything that comes into contact with it. It's the "axis mundi," that center around which the company's world and each individual can organize. Once leaders find solid ground from which they can confidently pivot, they're off to a great start. A "north star" orientation emerges around which the company and its employees can filter information and organize and focus their individual and collective activities. This sense of a unifying strategic clarity does not come easily. Once established, however, it is as solid as granite.

So 34 care centers in 17 states in two months. Several hundred, if not a thousand, interviews and encounters with everyone and anybody who had an opinion or worked with Amedisys. Some phenomenal road food. Meals that included red flannel hash, barbecue of all types, cornmeal and rice, crawfish, cheesesteaks, Chicago dogs, lobster rolls, soft-shell crab, gumbo—the list goes on . . .

The hotels were another story, particularly in small towns. Very Spartan on a good day. I made some friends by buying six-packs, sitting and sharing beer with my motel neighbors outside our motel rooms. It was a lot of fun, and some of my beer buddies even had strong opinions on home health. Every encounter provided an opportunity for learning something.

So after two months and multiple notebooks, I came back and boiled all the inputs down into core findings. The results became the strategic plan for our company. Amedisys would strive to do the following three simple but hard-to-accomplish objectives: (1) Deliver the best quality of care to our patients; (2) be the best place for caregivers to work; and (3) give our people the best tools so they can do the best job. If we did these three simple things well, Amedisys would grow—a lot!

This was and is the Amedisys strategy "of, by, and for the people," as Abraham Lincoln observed so eloquently about American government in his "Gettysburg Address." The power of giving a company over to its employees and customers is extraordinary. Not only do leaders get a better answer about what the company should be doing and how it should be doing it, but they also get a level of engagement and loyalty that generates exponential human, organizational, and financial returns.

When employees believe that they have a real stake in their company, that their voices and contributions matter, they will put extraordinary care and energy into their daily endeavors. They will surprise themselves and the company's leaders as they go above and beyond to delight and serve customers. Those referring patients will see the results and respond accordingly. They won't send their business anywhere else.

Whenever anyone at Amedisys, whether it's an aide in Alabama or a care center director in Maine, asks me quizzically why we do something, I invariably say something along the following lines:

This is your strategy, not mine. You're doing the work every day. I'm just holding up the mirror to the great work you're doing and trying to find ways to institutionalize it. You already know the answers; you know what's right and proper, what works and doesn't work. I'm asking: Please tell me what the right answer is, and if it's doable, then we'll try to do it.

And every year when we come back to revise and refresh our strategy, you (fellow employee) have the chance, opportunity, and obligation to tell me how to run the company better. I want your opinions. I want your voice. We need to know what we had gotten right and wrong as well as what needs to change. Tell us!

This is not a company run by a few oligarchs who lock themselves in a room and drink their own bathwater. The market told us what we needed, and our people on the front line told us what they needed to get us there. We had to constantly tune ourselves to the marketplace. Once we did, the more we listened and tuned in, the better the company did.

After I completed my walkabout, I returned to our cavernous Baton Rouge headquarters and used my notes to try to determine what type of culture was emerging. I became adamant that all our leaders needed to be in the field with our businesses as much as they could be, learning as much as they could about the care we deliver. Our subsequent success was a by-product of getting our corporate staff integrated with our field staff and their vital work. Not everyone got into the field as much as I did. I was a little manic about it. But my team, as I began assembling it, spent lots of time out learning our business firsthand.

Throughout my tenure at Amedisys, I tried to spend an average of one week a month in the field, visiting patients, caregivers, care centers, hospitals, and other post-acute facilities (which referred home care patients to us). It allowed me to see the whole spectrum of humanity under stress. It both grounded and shaped my executive leadership. I wanted and needed our corporate staff to have the same granular understanding of how our essential work manifested itself quietly and effectively in homes throughout the country.

Since I firmly believed that I really did know nothing, I was always interested in learning directly from our caregivers and our patients. The answers to turning our company around resided within our people, our patients, and our markets. We just had to know how to ask the right questions to find the right answers to unlock our potential.

After the walkabout, I came to the very firm belief that the corporate function exists to serve and aid our frontline staff. Going through the company's organizational chart and workflows, I realized that Amedisys was suffering from a major case of "founderitis" and its natural by-product: a hub-and-spoke organizational model.

Bill had started the company from scratch, and for over 30 years had built it up into a very successful company. One of the principal reasons that Amedisys floundered was that he never gave up the reins. He knew more about the company than anyone else because he had done everything. As the company grew ever larger, he hampered its performance because everything had to go through him. Totally understandable but deadly if growth is an objective.

In the small and early stages of a founder-based hub-and-spoke model, the company outperforms the market. The founder/CEO is involved in everything. There is excitement, passion, new frontiers, a fight for survival. New employees flock to this company because they want to change things and be next to the visionary who is doing it.

As the company grows and adds corporate functions, corporate activity moves further and further away from the core of the business. As that happens, the founding entrepreneur should delegate operational responsibilities to others and focus on institutionalizing the company's core values within a bigger, more complex organization. Sam Walton of Walmart was masterful at this. Yet most founder/entrepreneurs treat their company like their children. They simply can't let go. They keep holding on to things they shouldn't since they honestly believe they know best, which in most cases they do, but they can't do everything.

At a certain size and complexity, it becomes clear to almost everyone that no single person, no matter how knowledgeable, committed, and talented, can manage all aspects of the enterprise. Tragically, the founder/CEO is often blind to this obvious truth. Things start to get gummed up waiting for decisions from the person in the center of the hub. Performance starts to slide. Good people who want and have earned more autonomy to do their jobs leave. Those who remain are usually mediocre loyalists who personally benefit from the hub-and-spoke structure even if it's bad for the company. They are OK with always answering yes to the CEO and waiting for permission to do anything.

Ichak Adizes, a former professor of organization at UCLA, conducted several interesting studies on the life cycles of corporations. He created frameworks to identify where a company is in that evolution. These frameworks identified certain gating factors that will stall a company's progression if not addressed properly. Adizes also describes the type of leaders and leadership models needed to progress through these stages. What is so interesting about Adizes's work is how predictable companies' evolutions have become. Each stage of evolution has uniform characteristics and warning signs.

I've interacted with multiple hub-and-spoke organizations as a consultant and investor. The evolution of founder-based companies to larger, more matrix-driven meritocracies is very difficult to achieve. There are graveyards full of companies that didn't make the transition. When I arrived at Amedisys, the warning signs of hub-and-spoke failure were obvious: an inability to make decisions, no articulated strategic goals, a passive senior management team—all reflecting a waiting culture structured around a very strong and opinionated leader.

So we had to break Amedisys up and reconfigure its management model. In the process, I had to see if there was enough backbone and independence within the organization's leaders to stand up and compete on their own. It turned out that most of Amedisys's legacy leaders did not have the wherewithal to reinvent themselves. As a consequence, I replaced all the C-suite leaders I inherited and most of their direct reports.

If we were going to dig the company out of the hole that its founder had created, we had to create an organization with enough confidence to listen to our markets and our frontline employees when making strategic decisions. We ultimately did. It was a painful yet productive process that enabled us to upgrade our talent, distribute our work, and learn that wisdom emanates from the marketplace, not the CEO's office.

KEY TAKEAWAYS

- If you really want to understand your company, leave it for a while. Personally interact with the frontline employees who make and deliver the company's products and/or services as well as the customers who buy them. Visit former customers and others who are making purchases from your competitors. Find out why. Try to see your company from as many angles as you can. Create and encourage an open and safe environment for unfiltered feedback. Embrace and internalize both good and bad feedback.

- Corner offices are nice but sterile and one-dimensional. Staying in one place creates information bubbles characterized by homogenized information and feedback. Leaders often hear what they want to hear, not what they should hear. Create and foster as many information channels from as many angles as you can. Don't let your headquarters become a mausoleum. Homogenization is good for milk, not for receiving feedback.

- Don't develop products or services in a vacuum. Make sure the dogs want to eat the dog food you are making. "Should" logic never works in isolation. It gets trumped by the market's unanticipated vagaries. Marketplace dynamics are rarely logical. Develop products and services that people actually want. Listen to your end users. Design to their needs. Bring those with sales and production responsibility into the creation and evaluation processes. Better yet, if you can, let these people guide you.

- Always have people around you who will tell you the truth. Regardless of how bad the news or their criticism, take it in.

Then ask them to find solutions as well. Reward colleagues both for being truthful *and* for coming to the table with solutions.

- Be willfully ignorant like Socrates. Question base assumptions openly. Create environments for collectively understanding reality and change. Cultivate a solutions culture. Never "drink your own bathwater."
- Jostle up routine. Create experiences that inspire new insights by changing the scenery. Drink beer with strangers on the stoops of cheap motels. Be open and willing to learn out of context.
- Build your strategies with input from your customers and your employees. Invite as many stakeholders as you can to help form the company's strategic vision. Broad participation creates grounded strategies anchored and embraced by those who will drive the results. Spread ownership of purpose widely within your company.

4

TRIAL BY FLOOD

It was August 2016. A massive tropical storm was slamming into Baton Rouge. As the torrential rains subsided, I got a distressing call. Bill Borne, Amedisys's founder and my predecessor, was missing.

Just 20 months into my tenure as CEO, I was still wrestling to get a toehold in the organization. Despite heroic efforts including my walkabout, I still had not won our employees' hearts and minds.

We were doing better operationally and financially, but the company was still caught in a declining death spiral. As the company malingered, it was still trying to decide who was its true leader. I was a first-time Yankee CEO with no experience running a publicly traded company. I was competing for legitimacy against Bill's legend. Bill had been a very charismatic leader and his legacy still exerted enormous influence.

While the Amedisys board had pushed Bill to resign and he was trying to move on with his life, his presence and DNA were everywhere. Much of the organization was still loyal and indebted to him. Bill had created and built our wonderful company. Like most founder-run companies, the company's culture reflected its founder's personality. Bill was a huge, swashbuckling personality. Larger than life. The world was his for the taking. Bill ran Amedisys as a hub-and-spoke organization, with himself as the hub. Everything went through him. Bill started the organization from scratch, built it up over the years, and knew everything about it.

There were more stories about Bill's legendary feats than I could chronicle. I'm still hearing new ones today. Bill was what all our employees wanted—passionate, uncompromising, daring, and unyielding. He was always in the trenches with them, the very embodiment of a charismatic and visionary leader. Now he was missing.

On August 11, a large, slow-moving storm began heading toward Baton Rouge from Mexico. The city sits on the banks of the Mississippi River, an hour and a half northwest of New Orleans. As the storm approached, it magnified and became a "perfect storm" that hit Baton Rouge like a freight train. Meteorologists declared it a "once-in-500-year event."

The storm stalled north of Baton Rouge. Rain poured down for three days, dropping an average of 20 inches, and in the most extreme case 31 inches of rain. Baton Rouge is a relatively flat town surrounded by bayous with little elevation. Several Mississippi River tributaries in and around the city flooded badly. An unbelievable 7.1 trillion gallons of rainwater soaked the region. It was biblical. By contrast, Katrina dropped "just" 2.1 trillion gallons of rain on New Orleans in 2005.

The results were catastrophic. The city was completely flooded for days, parts of it for weeks. People had to be rescued from their homes. Everything was closed off. I was in Nashville and could not get into town. According to reports from the National Weather Service, 50,000 to 75,000 structures flooded and 13 people died. Several Amedisys employees showed me pictures of alligators and water moccasins perched on their patios and doorways. When the rains stopped and the floodwaters started to recede, Louisiana returned to its normal August weather, which is extremely hot and humid. Rot, mold, and mildew were everywhere. The stench in many places was overpowering.

A couple of days after the rains stopped, I arrived on the scene and began helping our people assess what had happened and see what the company could do to help them get their lives back on track. At the same time, the news that Bill was missing whipped through the company. With the deluge at full force, Bill had decided to check up on his property and his neighbors. He got on his all-terrain vehicle at 2 a.m., headed out into the storm, and never came back. His daughter posted messages in various media outlets saying he was missing and asking if anyone had seen him.

Volunteers searched for him everywhere. Rumors swirled around the office. "He was found clinging to a tree near Mallard Lakes," close to where he lived. "He had managed to escape the flood and was being rescued in (various high-ground outposts)." Please remember, this was Bill! He had faced far worse. A once-in-500-year storm was nothing. Tragically, rescuers found Bill's body several days later. Rising waters had swept Bill off his ATV. He drowned alone and in darkness.

The company was in shock. Despondent in many ways. I called the then-chairman of the board, Don Washburn. Don had been on the board for 15 years. He knew and loved Bill. He also had been instrumental in pushing for Bill's resignation, believing that the company needed new leadership and a different approach. I'd kept Don constantly informed of the events involving Bill as they unfolded. When I told him of Bill's death, he paused to recover his composure and then quietly said:

It's time for you to lead now. While horrible, Bill's presence and influence didn't allow you to lead this organization. Now if you handle this right, you can help the company repair itself and move forward. This organization has suffered serious trauma, and you have to be the one to lead it out of this mess and into the future. It's going to be really hard because you aren't Bill, but now that he's gone, they need you.

I took a deep breath. As usual, Don was spot-on. The company was drifting. The flood and Bill's demise had the potential to permanently rip Amedisys from its moorings, sending the company out to meander and sink in open water. We had to regain our footing. Healing and renewal had to begin immediately. We collectively needed to gain control of our future, or the company would collapse into chaos.

Many employees couldn't return to our offices in Baton Rouge after the flood. About a third had damaged homes. In many cases, lingering floodwaters prevented access and remediation. Schools, which normally open in August, stayed closed. Access to basic services and products was uneven. Stress levels were off the charts.

I wandered around our headquarters offices, listening to those people who made it in and trying to understand their pain and perspectives. Many were quite hostile, suggesting I or the company was responsible for Bill's death. These in-your-face, oft-shouted opinions were hard to hear, but authentic. I appreciated the brutal honesty.

I spent most of my time visiting affected employees in their homes. I wanted to understand firsthand what had happened and what our people were going through. Seeing the devastation and understanding their trauma was a heartbreaking revelation. The waters destroyed the first floors of most homes I visited. There was no clean water and no electricity in most places. Louisiana houses are built to keep the water out. They have to be, because once the elements sneak through a home's defenses, the damage can be devastating. It certainly was in this instance.

In house after house, there were piles of furniture, carpets, everything that could absorb water, sitting out on the side of the street for the garbage trucks to haul away. Couches, beds, books, photo albums—nothing could be saved. The heat and the water were eating everything up, but the people's resilience constantly amazed me. They were already at work, cleaning everything out of their houses, cutting out the affected drywall, running generators to power the fans that dried the sodden wood framing. They were doing supply runs for themselves and their neighbors, trying to get insurance on the line so they could start paying for supplies and repairs.

I get way too much undue credit for my role in helping our people recover. There were a couple of articles written in the *Wall Street Journal* about me, the company, and our response to the crisis. Many of our company leaders put as much effort as I did or more into helping our people. I focused on being a feeling human being, not a CEO. Seeing this devastation really shook me up. Several times between visiting houses, I had to pull over on the side of the road and collect myself. Seeing this level of unfairness and suffering happening to good people deeply unsettled me.

The company's collective response was remarkable. We took great care of our affected people, about 30 percent of our headquarters staff. To the extent I was helpful, it was in clearing the way for people to take care of each other. No idea or resource was spared or denied. Our supply chain people dug in to get the materials our people needed to get their houses clean and disinfected. Our supply chain people also sourced building materials and helped make repairs. Our legal team quickly shifted from handling corporate matters to helping our employees get their claims processed expediently and to apply for emergency aid.

Our finance team advanced funds to their affected colleagues, so they could pay their bills and cover incremental repair costs. We provided hotel rooms and meal vouchers for our displaced people. I got wads of cash from the bank and went shopping for supplies from legitimate and some questionable sources (hence the cash) and distributed them. I dispensed the money to people who would accept it. Few did. They accepted the supplies I bought more readily.

For the first time since I had arrived, Amedisys and I were focused on the same two goals—helping those who were afflicted by the catastrophic flood and getting the company going again. Fortunately, these circumstances played into my sweet spot: managing in a crisis, fighting like a bobcat with everything I had, doing what I believed was right for "my people." There were no debates, no hesitation. Until that time, I don't think either our people or even myself had thought of me leading in this manner. But after seeing what this hell unleashed on our company and people, my job was to close the door. The hammer had found its nail. After the flood, these were my people. They may or may not have liked me. I'm far from perfect. I have many flaws, but I was all in. Good luck to anyone who would get in our way. That's when everything changed.

I also needed to come to terms with Bill's legacy personally if I wanted to successfully lead the company he built from the ground up. Prior to his death, just his presence undermined me in various subtle ways that kept me from really taking hold and running the company. I tried to find pockets of support to tell my side of the story, to explain why Bill had to leave Amedisys and how important it was for the company to move beyond him.

On a human level, Bill's death gutted me. I did not care anymore about what he did or didn't do, about what damage he did to me or the company, or that in the eyes of many, I was not a worthy successor. Bill had been an enormously successful and charismatic leader. He had a family, friends, a community. In mourning his loss, I was able to meet them. Through his death, I was able to see and understand the man in full, more than simply a rival and an adversary.

I went to his memorial service. Most of the company was there. A couple of people told me I had a lot of nerve showing up. Bill's wife, Wendy, calmed things down. She was incredibly kind and welcoming. I was able to sit in a pew and thank Bill for what he had created. I understood how important it was for me to honor his legacy by taking care of our people, his and mine!

My appearance at Bill's memorial service turned out to be a watershed moment. By sitting alone in a pew with a bowed head, it showed Bill's true believers—his ardent supporters—that I could acknowledge his accomplishments. It showed that I honored and respected his legacy. My actions and demeanor demonstrated that I honored and respected his legacy. They showed that the new head of Amedisys, along with the other outsiders who had recently joined the company, needed and wanted to offer our respect and condolences. In subsequent talks with legacy employees, this seemed to be the moment when they decided that I was on their side and committed to building upon the culture of caregiving that Bill had created.

After the flood crisis subsided, I reflected on its extraordinary symbolism. Flood mythology is ubiquitous in creation myths: Hindu, Mesopotamian, Hebrew, Babylonian, the Cheyenne Indians, Greek, and Aboriginal tribes. It's everywhere. The most famous versions are the Epic of Gilgamesh and Noah's Ark. Not surprisingly, most of the early flood stories come from civilizations located near big rivers. In almost all cases, a god sends the floodwaters to annihilate and replace unworthy populations. Floods also signal rebirth, a time to start afresh and rebuild.

I think the flood metaphor was very apt for Amedisys. For me and the organization to move forward, we needed a dramatic clean start. The old antediluvian world must get subsumed and drown. A new world emerges to replace it. A flood is violent and cleansing at the same time. Destruction and renewal in the same package.

But having lived through this, let me assure you that the fresher the start you are given for renewal, the more commensurate pain and suffering you must experience. I did not expect or want so much drama and tragedy, but it came. I had to deal with it and try to channel it as best I could into something positive.

It jolted me and the company forward with such force and eventual clarity that we quickly aligned and became the excellent company of caregivers we are today. We had no choice. In a way, the flood made it much easier for all of us to move forward. And move forward we did.

After Bill's death, Amedisys needed a seeker with some grit to rewire its corporate circuitry. I was made for this purpose. We collectively had to get back on our feet, realign, and move forward with clarity, determination, and purpose. The shock of Bill's death created a tragic vision for the company and its people. It eliminated pretense and voided the corrosive effects of petty politics. Circumstances had shackled us together in a basement dungeon, but we had a choice. We could either wallow in our tragedy and let the company die or break our chains, crawl out of the dungeon, and show the world that the Amedisys story would not end in despair and defeat.

Escaping the basement dungeon required a forceful embrace of our corporate mission. We had to build something tangible out of the weakened and broken Amedisys shell. We'd seen behind the curtain. We got it. This was not the end of the Amedisys story. It was a new beginning. Our thinking represented the "neurobiology of hope" in action. Our collective neurons were firing. We said, "Let's rewire them and see what we've got." We changed the game, learned new rules, and played to win. And so we did.

KEY TAKEAWAYS

- A company cannot move into its future until it comes to terms with its past.
- Leaders can exploit adverse events to break down barriers and strengthen their companies. To forge new paths, engage in new dialogues, and rebuild stronger. Use your collective and shared adversity to invite and build participation, commitment, and loyalty.
- True mettle endures in hard times. Hard times present an opportunity to see your company and its people in a new, harsher light. Unvarnished views are always the most insightful. Watch and see which people thrive under duress.
- In hard times, your company and its people will be watching you closely and will remember everything you do. Do the right thing. Always.
- In the ruins of destruction are the seeds of renewal. Find and cultivate them, but never forget the place you came from because you don't want to go back.

5

PEOPLE POWER

One day as I was looking at our company's organizational chart, my first thought was, "This is completely wrong . . . ass backwards." When I turned it upside down, it suddenly made complete sense. Ideally, Amedisys should operate as an upside-down pyramid. At the top are our patients, next are our clinicians who deliver care directly to our patients, and after that are locally based teams that provide direct support to frontline caregivers.

Following those top-three tiers are regional care center managers and business development liaisons. These professionals solicit and coordinate patient referrals and transfers. Next are the business-line leaders who manage the company's divisions. At the bottom is me. This made total sense. I was the furthest from our actual delivery of care. My C-suite executives were also far removed from patient care delivery. We might have the fancy titles and highest salaries, but we had the least actual influence in driving high-quality care services for the 65,000 patients the company served every day.

I wanted to circulate my "new and improved" organizational chart widely within the company. I even had our graphics department create a funny organizational chart, with me looking up at all the layers above me. Despite my best efforts, this never happened. Trying to protect me, our communications team buried my concept and funny chart. It never saw the light of day. Even without a new organizational chart, I believe that service businesses, such as Amedisys, should acknowledge the primacy of frontline operations. That is where the company generates its real value—with patients.

There is an obvious but unspoken truth at healthcare services companies like Amedisys: There would be no company without patients and frontline caregivers. I do not mean to diminish the roles and incredible value that corporate functions can deliver. The company needs corporate expertise and functions to manage at scale, but they are there solely to serve operations by keeping them compliant, helping track and benchmark performance, making sure they hire the best people, reporting the numbers correctly, and so on.

That being said, privileged corporate officers like me should have a broader, more comprehensive enterprise view. It should encompass all constituents, including employees, patients, shareholders, insurers, the government, and regulatory agencies. Corporate's primary role is to allocate resources effectively, settle disputes, and manage trade-offs, all for the greater good of the enterprise and the value it creates for customers. Above all, leaders like me should always realize that the guts of healthcare services work manifest in the field in core operations, not at the corporate offices. The essential work happens visit by visit, day by day, care center by care center.

If you're sensing a theme or a pattern here, well done. As we soldiered through the Amedisys turnaround, we discovered that delegating responsibility for deciding operational strategies to those with direct experience and a personal stake in the outcome was a proven recipe for success. The bigger the group of people helping me make the decisions, the better; the more, the merrier. When I relied on corporate professionals lacking firsthand operational knowledge and direct patient experience to make strategic operational decisions, execution and outcomes suffered. Out-of-touch corporate types would leap way too far and miss the mark. The assumptions driving their decision-making were often inaccurate, even incorrect.

The only way corporate leaders can truly succeed in healthcare services is by spending a significant portion of their time directly seeing and experiencing care operations. Better yet, participating in them. I can't deliver clinical care when I'm in a patient's house, but I can take notes, ask questions, fetch things, observe the environment. By participating in the visit, I can develop the firsthand knowledge required to make better strategy and resource allocation decisions.

As CEO, my job evolved and ultimately became one of trying to create a culture of engaged listening that allowed those most affected by a problem to work on it and attempt to solve it. It was my job to find and enable the right people who could work the problem and then support them with the right resources and best problem-solving tools. As leaders, we can give them the time and resources to help them. We can give them methods and analytical tools to help them frame challenges appropriately. Once the delegated team derives its answers, we can institutionalize the team's findings and solutions. We can spread that knowledge through the organization.

Most of my initial work centered on creating a culture of trust where our people could express themselves without fear of retaliation. We wanted and needed people's honest and unvarnished feedback. The old culture operated top-down rather than bottom-up. By setting the example for other leaders that spending my time out learning and listening was vitally important to the company's future, I felt our people would understand and appreciate the importance of our core operations. If CEO Paul is listening, learning, and finding workable solutions to our problems, then maybe we all should try to do the same.

Next I had to put in place structures by which we could receive feedback efficiently. Encouraging it was one thing, but it has to have guardrails. As I became known as the CEO who was always out there and always responsive, I became deluged. In response, I became better at picking my spots, strategically reaching out to select people to deliver targeted messages. But the message never changed. Amedisys is a listening and learning organization where we value all voices, where we encourage and consider all reasonable feedback. Act accordingly.

The company itself is highly decentralized and organized geographically around its care centers. Care centers consist of clinicians, clinical managers, business office managers, business development staff, and sales liaisons. Larger centers also included schedulers, billers, coordinators, and clinical aides.

At care centers offering hospice services, staff also includes chaplains, bereavement counselors, social workers, and volunteer coordinators. Amedisys's care centers range in size generally from 10 to 40 people, the average size being in the mid-20s.

The official title for individuals leading our care centers is director of operations (DOO). The most important leaders at Amedisys are our DOOs. They are the CEOs of the company's care centers. Care centers with effective DOOs thrive. Those with ineffective DOOs suffer. Getting effective DOOs at all of the company's 550 care centers is a big but doable challenge. Nothing is more important. As Amedisys improves the caliber and performance of its DOOs, which it is doing, the company will prosper.

Most DOOs have not received formal training in business management. They are generally ex-clinicians/nurses who excelled at delivering great patient care. That is the most important thing a care center can do—deliver great care to its patients.

But delivering great care and managing great care delivery require very different skill sets. It's an age-old challenge in business. The best individual performers don't always become the best leaders. A great clinician uses his or her medical knowledge and experience in care delivery to diagnose and manage patients through their episodes. A great manager facilitates all facets of great care; keeps the clinicians scheduled, on track, and engaged; makes sure that the supporting functions are working; and ensures that the whole spectrum of care from referral to discharge across the full patient panel is operating efficiently.

DOOs have to be very good operators/managers in a complex care delivery system. A typical DOO at Amedisys manages 15 clinicians across a 220+ patient census. This requires training. Again, not rocket science. The most important performance improvement lever within Amedisys is upgrading the caliber of our DOOs. We need to make our 550 DOOs the best managers they can be. We need to help them transform themselves into healthcare business leaders who can manage a clinical care business consisting of hard-to-find, skilled professionals. Reducing turnover of essential frontline staff is what most differentiates great DOOs.

In order to complete 65,000 visits a day and still grow our business, Amedisys needs licensed, skilled clinicians who can go into someone's home and deliver appropriate care services better than anyone else. When broken down to its studs, Amedisys is basically a staffing business. What do good staffing businesses need?

First and foremost, they need to hire and keep great people! This requires a culture where employees want to make a career working for Amedisys. The longer clinical staff practice within our company, the better and more productive they become. Our DOOs needed to become better at recruiting and retaining talent. We needed to help them learn how to do this.

Second, DOOs need logistical tools to optimize clinical staff time without burning them out. A key tool in home care management is the center's EMR (electronic medical record). It records the home visit in its entirety. It is essential for capturing patient's health status and billing. While vital, using EMRs should not be burdensome. All logistical tools need to be mutually beneficial. A good EMR should not only get the information the company needs, it also should make clinical documentation easy to compile and complete. Most importantly, it should create an individualized patient narrative to coordinate that patient's care delivery and drive better care outcomes.

Third and most important, health services companies need to create a culture of caring for all who engage with it. This includes patients, employees, families, and partners. Caring for others manifests in multiple ways. It is a frame of mind. It requires empathy and a proactive approach to problem solving. Engaged employees incorporate caring into their daily work. Done consistently, it elevates their sense of purpose at work and rubs off on others. When employees adopt a caring mindset, results get exponentially better.

Back to Amedisys's DOOs. From what I have seen, about a third of our DOOs have progressed or evolved into their managerial roles naturally. About half of our DOOs have the potential to become great managers but need training, oversight, and consistent feedback. The remaining 15+ percent of DOOs struggle. More often than not, this group uses heavy-handed management tactics to promote effective caregiving. Those tactics never work. These DOOs push their clinicians the way their managers pushed them when they were line nurses or physical therapists. Over time, Amedisys needs to replace the DOOs it cannot re-acculturate. Shifting to nonclinical care managers is not a workable long-term solution. The clinical and business office expertise bar needed in care delivery is quite high. Nonclinical managers are often ill-equipped to address clinical and patient care issues. Some nonclinical managers can succeed as DOOs, but this is rare.

So the key for Amedisys is making our DOOs the best managers possible. In addition to more intense management training for new DOOs, I would put myself on their learning agenda. I'd call each newly promoted DOO once a month. I would also lead in-person training sessions for all incoming DOOs. I do not know the specifics of running a care center, but I do know that having the CEO spend an hour listening to their fresh-eyed perceptions, sharing my observations, detailing keys for success, and answering their questions makes a big impression. It should. I want them to know their importance to the company.

Most new DOOs, particularly those recruited from other companies, have never met their CEOs. My message to new DOOs is quite clear. I congratulate them on getting the job. Then I tell them how important their role is not only for the company but for their direct reports and their patients. Then I tell them what success looks like, what great DOOs do. I also highlight the workplace behaviors and characteristics of DOOs who fail.

The bottom line, I tell them, is turnover. People vote with their feet. If employees are leaving your care center, you've lost their vote. I suggest that they transfer the care focus they had for patients to their clinicians. I tell them:

> You won't be seeing patients anymore, but your people are the ones who need to know what good care looks like, and you can show them. So it's really not a big leap. Take the care you lavished on your patients and give it to your people. Listen, learn, assess, and build solutions to help them get where they need to go. Step in to help if needed. Have their backs.
>
> Watch what this does. If you do this—if you help them, nurture them, communicate with them, support them— you will be an enormous success. Transfer the care, take what you have so successfully done and redirect it. It's a directional change, not a big leap!

Once I give them this message, I then try to be a good example by shutting up and listening. I want my own behaviors to reflect the importance Amedisys places on being a listening and learning organization.

Our renewed focus on DOOs worked very well. It's reflected in the marked improvement in the performance of our care centers. The lesson here for CEOs is find the most important driver of your company's success and get very involved in elevating its performance. Giving our DOOs attention from the top, showing them what success looks like, and helping them get there are essential steps to improve the individual care center and overall organizational performance. This again is Golden Rule management in practice. Train your people well, give them the resources they require to succeed, and trust them to deliver superior outcomes for both customers and the company.

In addition to becoming a listening organization, we created something called "Solution Sessions" as a vehicle for upgrading the company's internal capabilities. On my own, I was trying to build pockets of expertise within our company to work on specific problems. It wasn't catching on and that was frustrating me. I would identify a problem, gather some subject-matter experts, have a call, ask them a bunch of questions, thank them profusely, and send them thank you notes and follow-ups, but these sessions ended up being dead sessions. Nothing much got accomplished. Time to go back to the drawing board.

Our head of communications, Kendra Kimmons, sensed my frustration. She suggested a broader approach. Voilà! Solution Sessions were born and they have taken off. Kendra sees almost everything that happens within our organization. She started to design these sessions by teeing up a problem and inviting interested people for conference calls to solve the problem. She capped the sessions at about 50 people. If a session was oversubscribed, she would schedule

another so everyone who wanted to had the opportunity to participate. She always had a good curator to lead the call, someone inviting and nonthreatening. The curator would ask for advice, receive
it, summarize it, and detail next steps. When complete, the curator
would issue a report on what had and had not gotten done.

Wisdom of the crowds works. I listened to several calls. They
were magical. People who had never found a way to contribute to
their company were now able to do so. The information we gleaned
from our Solution Sessions was rich and revealing. Not surprising really, since they represented another "of, by, and for the people" approach to problem solving. More often than not, the solutions
developed during the sessions worked. Why? Because the people solving the problems were the ones living with them.

The other tangential, and I would say equally important, benefit
was how Solution Sessions enriched and enlivened our corporate culture. Participants told their colleagues about how the company was
asking their advice and wanted to hear what they had to say. The beneficial impact compounded as word spread through the ranks. These
engaged employees emphasized that management wanted to hear
from them, that their opinions and knowledge mattered, and that
they could make Amedisys a better company. We told them, "Thank
you for helping us and in turn helping you, your colleagues, and our
patients." Our messaging had to be a real and meaningful program to
earn our employees' trust and engagement. It was. The worst thing an
organization can do is ask for employee input and then ignore it. As
always, the Golden Rule applies.

We reviewed and updated our strategy every year. Since the
pandemic, the healthcare marketplace has changed considerably.
COVID has been a double-edged sword, positive in many ways and
devastating in other ways. As COVID demonstrated, market dynamics are ever-changing. That's why it is important that we constantly

ask ourselves whether we are on the right track. So every year we take what we are hearing, build up a strawman strategy, test it out with our people, revise it, get approval and input, and then break it down into tangible pieces for a trackable work plan.

As a trained strategist, I made sure that Amedisys took its strategic planning process very seriously. Good strategies create a tight and focused organization that knows why it's here and what it's supposed to do. Good strategic planning enhances a company's culture by reinforcing its core values and applying them in a forward-thinking, market-oriented way that creates value for customers and drives success.

For Amedisys, strategy is an ongoing, inclusive process. We constantly stress-test our plan, checking and rechecking it. We look for new ideas, market events, new technologies, and whatever else there may be to see if any of these things knock us off our block and/or if we need to incorporate any of them into our existing strategy.

We also take everything we've learned and construct a preliminary strawman presentation. We first vet that presentation deck with the broader management team. After that, we take our strawman strategy to the board for a long discussion. After the board agrees, we redraft the plan and take it out to the company, to the people who will have to make it work. They tweak it and tell us what's real and what isn't. Then we take our strategy and break it down into tangible actions, and then we set up tracking mechanisms so we constantly know how we are doing. If a strategy cannot be boiled down to specific actions and tangible, trackable results, it will be ineffectual. All this ongoing input goes into finalizing the plan.

A board is responsible to the shareholders for a company's strategic direction. So once the Amedisys board signs off on the company's final strategy, leadership needs to sell the strategy to the rest of the company. We particularly engage our operating personnel who have to turn our strategy into reality. We need everyone on board. In this way, a great strategic plan becomes a companywide work plan. The parts support the whole. Everyone becomes responsible for implementing the plan and tracking its success.

Before finalizing our strategy for board review and approval, we fly in dozens of our colleagues to critique and "finish off the half-baked loaf." The plan does not become final until the managers who have to execute the strategy get a chance to see it, debate it, give us their feedback, and help us adjust the plan if necessary. They tell us what it's going to take to get there. They wrangle over resources, debate the probabilities of success, and tweak the timing of the deliverables. It's a wonderful time. By the end of this full-contact process, we collectively have a strategic plan that we agree on, believe in, and think is achievable. A good plan always includes some ambitious "stretchers" that will be hard goals to achieve. It should be hard to hit stretch targets.

Once the plan goes final, my work really begins. I boil down the strategy presentation, then hit the road and the phone lines. My objective is to review our strategic plan with all our employees. I want them to hear it from me, and I want to ask for their support. I want them to know that they are essential to making the plan work. I take the time to walk them through it, take questions, and debate objections if necessary. What I like about this process won't surprise any readers who have gotten this far. It's not *my* strategy. It's *everybody's* strategy. I encourage all our leaders to own the strategy and sell it directly to their people. Why do I do this? For a great strategic plan to work, all the company's employees need to believe it's theirs as well as mine.

So a great strategy embodies a company's credo. It amplifies its "I believe" values. It restates and animates the company's purpose and what the company stands for. I've learned over the years that the only way a strategy can become a transformative journey is with everyone on board. The way to get universal buy-in is by bringing everyone in, listening, learning, adjusting, and finally creating a plan that invites everyone's participation. There will be those who are not all in, who don't want to climb the hill. It's time to thank them and send them elsewhere.

Another thing I've learned about strategy is that it's never fixed. It's always fluid. Like the ancient Greek philosopher Heraclitus said, "You never step into the same river twice." The only constant is change. Strategic frameworks require constant tinkering and readjusting. Good companies execute well on what they can control and adapt to what they cannot. These are the table stakes. A good strategy development process helped Amedisys become a good company.

A great company takes the surprises it can't control and reacts better and faster than its competitors. It turns "good" challenges into opportunities as fast as it possibly can. This is hard to do, but great companies do it. Problems and setbacks are inevitable. Facing them squarely and honestly is the key to finding and implementing solutions. By embracing the problem and diving into it, companies turn a negative into a positive. Diving into problems might seem reckless. It's not. Since problems do not go away, avoiding them and delaying action only digs a deeper hole. Finding solutions to problems earlier than your competition creates a competitive advantage. It also removes that psychic drag that plagues an organization that tries to avoid what is inevitable.

It's important to convey how the Amedisys strategic planning process works and how it drove us to the many successes we achieved during my tenure as CEO. I have no doubts there is enormous potential to further improve and grow the company as we move toward achieving our three strategic goals: Provide great care for patients; be the best place for caregivers to work; and give our people the resources they need to succeed.

Great strategy unleashes people power. It's nuclear! Market-driven strategies that work come from the people who deliver, receive, buy, and provide our products. Amedisys operates six lines of business: home health, hospice, a personal care network, hospital at home, SNF at home, and palliative care. Over 90 percent of our business resides in home health and hospice services. The other product lines are nascent; they represent the company's future but haven't scaled yet. This is a classic S-curve market opportunity (see Figure 5.1): Run the core, mature businesses efficiently; build the new businesses up in the background so they're ready to step to the fore when their market opportunity arrives.

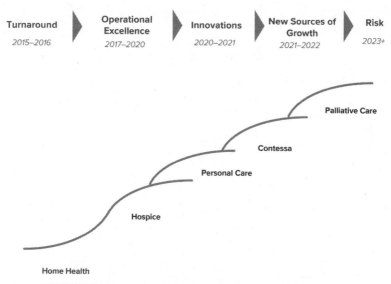

FIGURE 5.1   A company's S-curve depicts how it uses revenues from its existing businesses to fund its future business in a sequential fashion.

Absent externalities, the S-curve governs market dynamics in a Darwinian manner. The inevitability of innovation and the relentless nature of competition require constant business model adaptation for economic survival. S-curves are a good way to show that growth trajectories are not inevitable. Companies must prepare for the time when their core products start to decline. They must have investment strategies that enhance longer-term competitiveness as market dynamics shift. It's a relentless, infinite game that spans multiple leadership teams within successful organizations. With innovation and focus, successful companies survive by developing new products that meet evolving market demands.

When I started at Amedisys, we were primarily a home health company. Over the years, we built up our hospice presence to become the third best provider in the United States. Our other businesses are expanding the company's capacity to take care of more and sicker people in their homes. The common theme that runs through all our businesses is that we take care of people in their homes. That is where more and more patients will receive their care. At Amedisys, we will continue to look for better and better ways to provide this care to the growing number of Americans who want it.

KEY TAKEAWAYS

- Look at and structure your organization in ways that are both truthful and aspirational. Organize your company to deliver value where it's most needed, now and forever.
- Direct all your company's energies and resources to move the performance needle in the places where it most matters.
- Honest feedback is the lifeblood of an organization. Cultivate a culture of trust that welcomes the truth and encourages unvarnished feedback. Constantly seek to understand how your employees, customers, partners, vendors, and the overall market view your company and its products. All the answers to a company's strategic issues, questions, and challenges are available to leaders who listen.
- Focus on the frontline employees who deliver products and services to customers. More often than not, truth comes from the line. Find ways to amplify their voices. If they have the right resources, skills, and capabilities, they can deliver transformative performance.
- Good strategy requires focus and definition. It articulates your organization's aspirations out loud. It then breaks these aspirations down into tangible, achievable tasks.
- Make the strategic planning process inclusive. Involve everyone. Make all employees believe they own a piece of the dream. Inclusiveness exponentially increases the odds of success. When everyone gets involved, everyone is an owner and has a stake in making the strategy become a reality.
- Great strategy harnesses your employees' collective will.

- The S-curve model shows the importance of constantly trying to find new ways to pivot, change, upgrade, and/or disrupt existing businesses.
- A leader's job is to preach the strategy and tell the story so it strikes a chord and resonates with everyone who hears it.
- Great companies address big problems up front and turn their solutions into competitive advantage. Weaker companies dodge problems and whither from indecisiveness.
- Hard problems are the biggest privilege any leader can have. These problems are what others can't or won't solve. Work them and create unique and surprising opportunities.
- Strategy is a full-time, all-encompassing job. It's a CEOs primary job, but you'll need help. Hire well. I did. Amedisys's current Chief Strategy Officer (CSO), Nick Muscato, constantly finds ways to incorporate the company's strategy into its daily workflows. This makes our strategy vital and exciting.

6

HOME IS WHERE THE CARE IS

The home is where much more care can and should be provided. Unfortunately, the current payment system for healthcare services directs a disproportionate amount of care into higher-cost facilities that deliver the same or inferior outcomes. From a cost perspective, institution-based care is three to eight times more expensive than equivalent home-based care. Equally important, patients prefer home-based care when it is available.

Other advanced economies understand home care's relative benefits. They direct a much higher percentage of care into the home. That is among the reasons that US care costs are much higher than other OECD (Organisation for Economic Co-operation and Development) countries. Despite the higher cost, the United States compares unfavorably with these countries on health status measures. This leads to a sobering conclusion. Higher care costs do not translate into better care outcomes. Americans deserve better.

There are way too many hospital beds in the United States and way too much hospital and institutional lobbying power driving care unnecessarily into expensive acute care settings. Hospitals represent significant employers in large to midsize US towns and cities. They have strong proponents in state and local governments. Hospitals use their considerable political and economic clout to maintain this unacceptable status quo.

Our current configuration of healthcare delivery and payment represents a twentieth-century solution to a twenty-first-century problem. The nature of disease has changed radically during the last 40 years. The Centers for Disease Control estimates that 90 percent of healthcare expenditures fund the care of individuals with chronic and mental health conditions. America is a country of chronically ill people, hampered by an expensive "sick care" delivery system that prioritizes institutional treatment (think hospitals) of individuals with acute illnesses. Prevention and chronic disease management are an afterthought. Effective treatment for chronic conditions occurs in community and home-based settings to minimize the need for institutionalized care.

In the 1980s, acute diseases consumed the majority of healthcare expenditure. Most costs originated from treatments for acute episodes. This equates to a very radical and fast transformation of the nature of illness and disease in our country. The medical care system has not properly acknowledged and addressed the predominance of chronic disease today. Consequently, the US health system centers on hospital-based care. This represents an expensive anachronism. Operating on an outdated institution-centric platform is unnecessarily bankrupting the country.

As a home care company, Amedisys is well positioned to accommodate the future movement of healthcare services into lower-cost and more convenient settings (including the home), assuming that the government and commercial payers eventually do what's best for their constituents and members. Guiding and incentivizing care toward the most effective sites of care will generate higher-quality outcomes at lower costs. Failure to redirect care in this manner would be catastrophic for the country. The current hospital and institutionally driven care delivery model is financially unsustainable. Continuing to rely on it will break the system. But "chicken" is a game we love to play in the United States—waiting until we are standing on the precipice before we are forced to pivot—so we'll see if logic prevails.

US demographics are also changing significantly. Our country is aging rapidly. That means that a larger and larger portion of the population will become chronically ill and need greater access to healthcare services. Institutionalized care has become proficient at keeping sicker people alive longer at high cost and a reduced quality of life.

There is also a psychographic element at work. For the next 20 to 30 years, the portion of the population that will need the most care does not want it in institutions. In 2023, the ages of this baby boom generation range between 59 and 77 years old. The onset of acute chronic disease generally happens when people are in their mid-60s, so there are already and will soon be more people needing clinical care. As many as 9 out of 10 baby boomers want to age in their homes and avoid institutional settings. They are 21 percent of the population but have over 53 percent of the wealth.

Counter to its own and the American people's interest, the US government has stymied this trend toward greater home-based care delivery. Since 2009, the Centers for Medicare and Medicaid Services (CMS) has lowered its payments for home health in aggregate by almost 40 percent. These cuts have been offset somewhat by annual market-basket (i.e., inflation) increases with the net effect being negative 17 percent. CMS and state governments fund approximately half of all healthcare costs through Medicare and Medicaid programs. CMS determines the payment formularies for Medicare-funded programs. The agency's aggressive payment cuts have been devastating to the home care industry. Continued underfunding will most likely drive more home health agencies out of business, particularly the small ones serving patients in rural and low-income areas.

In 2022, CMS proposed reduced payments for home health-care services by 7 percent, equally split between 2023 and 2024. Approximately a quarter of home care providers are currently operating at a breakeven performance. Another quarter have operating margins less than Medicare's proposed 7 percent rate cut. Payment cuts of this magnitude devastate the industry and limit access to the cost-effective home health services the public increasingly wants. The cut in home care reimbursement contrasts with large proposed percentage-rate increase during 2023 and 2024 for other types of care delivery, including hospital care. These payment decisions by Medicare are counterproductive and maddening. They occur under both Democratic and Republican administrations. Perplexing healthcare payment policies are a bipartisan failure.

Paradoxically the government's dated and ham-handed approach to its pricing of healthcare benefits creates a tremendous long-term benefit to Amedisys. The home health industry is highly fragmented. For many years, CMS artificially propped up home care providers via a "prepaid" government reimbursement system that paid 60 percent of care costs up front. In other words, CMS paid 60 percent of total home care costs before providers delivered any services—amazing! This essentially funded small home health businesses that did not have sufficient working capital.

This up-front payment methodology also enticed fraudulent players into the home care business. These bad actors would create fake home care companies, bill the government, and skip town without caring for any patients. Their behavior has tainted the home care industry and has been a contributing factor in Medicare's substandard home care payment rates. As part of its newest home care payment scheme initiated in 2019, CMS no longer prepays for home care services. This scheme eliminates the opportunity for bad actors to game the Medicare reimbursement system through fraudulent startups.

Heavy home care reimbursement cuts will trigger a large industry shakeout. This will benefit large, national players like Amedisys with access to capital. This shakeout will drive industry consolidation as smaller companies join the bigger home care organizations, and as many exit the business altogether. The people who will suffer most are those who lose access to home health services. Circumstances will force them to seek care in higher-cost institutional settings. This grim reality hurts these unfortunate Americans even as this redirected care depletes the Medicare trust fund and pushes it closer to insolvency.

Back to Amedisys. When I returned to the corporate offices after my walkabout, I had developed very strong ideas about where Amedisys needed to focus to turn its operations around. Amedisys's hub-and-spoke operating model caused the company's C-suite executives to lose touch with what the company did every day. Even worse, they became willfully ignorant of the many ways in which the company delivered true value-based care to its patients.

When I did my walkabout, I was delighted to discover that buried under all the corporate folderol was the company's ability to consistently deliver high-quality care. Eureka! Clinical excellence was the solid ground on which we could collectively revive the company. There was so much to do. I didn't think Amedisys was very good at operations and certainly not technology. Business development and sales were weak. The company wasn't growing. Compliance was a problematic—look at the $150 million fine we paid to the government. The market hated us and had put lots of "sells" and "holds" on our stock. Our work environment was toxic, with employee turnover exceeding 40+ percent.

Despite all these issues, I found that disproportionately Amedisys was a company of caregivers. We understood how, but still didn't always deliver great care in the home. Relative to the company's other challenges, however, clinical "fixes" related to patient care were the easiest. They were intuitive to our company, part of Amedisys's DNA. As we removed the obstacles to delivering great care, I felt our quality-of-care delivery would improve very quickly.

Needless to say, I guessed right. The No. 1 aim embedded in our strategic plan was to become the home care industry's highest-quality provider of clinical care services. Be the ones that took the best care of patients. So we looked very closely and evaluated the rules on how the government rated care delivery and went all-in on quality. We developed tracking tools. We rewarded care centers and clinicians that delivered great care. I wrote notes and cards to 5-star (the highest rating in the Medicare Star Ratings system) clinicians and care center DOOs. We made posters (Figure 6.1) celebrating 5-star achievements. Our chief nursing officer created a quality-monitoring and -tracking system to report activities and outcomes in close to real time.

Achieving great quality was so important to me and our company that I established a board committee to track and assure that we progressed to becoming the industry's best provider. The board incentivized us with equity grants and bonuses to hit our aggressive quality targets. We established a pool of bonus money to distribute to those individuals and centers that achieved the highest marks in quality. I spent much of my time visiting the care centers that delivered the best results, trying to isolate their best practices and then transfer them to lower-performing care centers. We were all in this together to create a culture of clinical care excellence. So I also went to the worst-performing care centers to identify, understand, and eliminate obstacles that kept them from becoming high-quality providers.

FIGURE 6.1 We did everything we could imagine to recognize and celebrate care centers that achieved 5-star ratings. This included posters for high-performing centers.

For the poor performers, two recurring themes emerged. First, these centers had stone-handed DOOs who struggled to motivate and manage people. This we could address. Second, these centers tended to operate in monopolistic markets where hospitals and other facilities used their market clout to direct patient referrals to preferred home care companies (usually owned by them). These market-specific factors limited our growth even if we were doing everything right. Together, these conditions resulted in high levels of employee turnover and a downward spiral in operating performance and quality. Accelerated turnover in a service provider company reliant on its people is a recipe for failure.

That's the other thing we learned. Turnover is the key to our business. If there is one metric that matters most, it is turnover. Luckily, I have been obsessed with turnover ever since I got into healthcare. There is a shortage of nurses and other clinicians. Nurses are coming to their retirement ages at an alarming rate, and they are not being replaced by enough new nurses. The demand for home-based clinicians is skyrocketing. Supply cannot keep up with demand. This is why attracting and retaining clinicians is essential to Amedisys's long-term success. There are some technology and staffing tools that we can use to improve clinician efficiency and productivity, but the macro employment factors make our situation even worse if we can't hold on to our own clinicians. Reducing turnover became my mantra.

Believe it or not, it is hard to calculate the cost of clinician turnover. Amedisys's finance professionals largely ignored turnover costs because they are not directly traceable. I disagreed and created a very rough formula for measuring the effect of turnover costs on Amedisys's financial performance. That impact was massive.

Presently Amedisys generates roughly $250 million in EBITDA (earnings before interest, taxes, depreciation, and amortization) on approximately $2.3 billion in annual revenues. That means our total cash expenses are just over $2 billion. And 85 percent of our costs relate to personnel. That's $1.75 billion. Post-COVID turnover rates are approximately 20 percent. We estimate that the company loses about a year's worth of an employee's revenue power when the person departs. I think the amount is actually higher, but let's stick with the more conservative assumption. That means turnover currently costs us over $300 million annually. So if we had no turnover, the company's cash flow would increase by over $300 million. Zero turnover is impossible, but cutting turnover in half would deliver $150+ million in additional income to the bottom line. Conversely, if Amedisys had reverted to its old 40+ percent turnover rate, the company would have lost over $700 million. When analysts ask how Amedisys's margins during my tenure grew from below 6 percent to 14 percent, I tell them that reducing turnover was the driving force.

Reducing turnover has an expansive compounding benefit. Beyond the lower costs of onboarding new clinicians as turnover rates declined, Amedisys also improved productivity and utilization rates as fewer employees turned over. It makes sense. The fewer people who leave, the longer the average employee tenure grows, and the better and more efficient employees become at their jobs. Clinician productivity increased by double digits for several years as the company's efforts to improve employee retention took hold. The same people with the same workload, only doing the work much more efficiently. We measured how each additional year of clinician tenure drove better results in cost, productivity, utilization, use of other resources in the company, and, most importantly, better patient outcomes.

We analyzed turnover rates by care center. Leadership matters. The strongest predictor of turnover rates at specific care centers was the quality of the DOO. Within a decentralized service delivery company like Amedisys, strong local leadership and a supportive culture are key. Knowing this narrowed my strategic focus to making sure we had superlative leaders at each of the company's 550 care centers. If we could do that, most other incremental strategies would be much easier to implement.

There was another important relationship we discovered that fueled the company's turnaround and subsequent prosperity. Growth was directly correlated to our star or patient care/quality ratings. Patients flocked to care centers with higher Medicare Star Ratings. At the time, if a care center achieved 5 stars, the highest possible, its average growth rate was 6–7 percent, double the industry average of 3 percent. At 4.5 stars, the average growth rate dropped to 5–6 percent. At 4 stars, growth averaged 4–5 percent. Less than 4 stars had 3 percent growth, which is the industry average.

CMS manages the government's star rating program and is constantly adjusting and raising its performance levels to drive the industry toward better care delivery. When I was at Humana, higher star ratings for Medicare Advantage plans triggered performance bonuses from the government. This is a form of value-based care. That mechanism is coming soon to the home health and hospice sectors. High-quality care already correlates with higher growth rates in volume. Soon it also will lead to additional revenue growth for performance bonuses. Accordingly, the best home care providers will grow faster and will earn higher margins. Emphasizing quality is the right thing to do. This is very good news for Amedisys.

The professionals who refer patients to home care providers are doctors, nurses, hospitalists, discharge planners, case managers, and clinicians in SNFs, ALFs, IRFs, and ILs. Most of these people are clinicians and understand the importance of high-quality service provision. Consequently, they disproportionately refer more patients to higher-quality providers so that "their" patients receive the highest quality of care.

Is there unfairness in the system? Absolutely, particularly when hospital systems own home health companies and drive patients into their facilities. This occurs routinely even though hospitals are notoriously ineffective at running home health and hospice agencies.

Having run hospital, home health, and hospice businesses throughout my career, I can affirm that they are very different entities. In many markets where hospitals predominate, they expand their presence and diversify their revenues by buying or starting ancillary services, including home health and, less often, hospice. Amedisys sometimes get passed over in favor of inferior home health and hospice providers owned by hospital systems.

Is steering business unethical? Of course, but it happens. These artificial constraints are unlikely to last as healthcare markets become more competitive and transparent. As we've discussed, it is safer and better to dive deep into your core strengths to drive incremental value than to reach outside of them. The healthcare business is complicated enough. The companies that stick to their swim lanes rather than sloppily try to expand into new business lines, even when they have market clout, tend to do better.

The other thing we found is that as companies excel in specific business sectors, opportunities to expand into tangential parts of that sector emerge. We viewed this like earning dessert by cleaning your plate. We have worked hard to excel at our core home health and hospice businesses, to become the industry's best provider in these sectors. So Amedisys only expanded into "close-to-the-core" businesses where our core businesses enabled us to use and leverage existing organizational capabilities. We also found that these close-to-the-core businesses enhanced and complemented the core businesses. So we got a twofer by expanding into new markets while creating incremental value for our complementary core businesses.

A good example of close-to-the-core expansion for Amedisys is hospice. During my walkabout to our home healthcare centers, many mentioned their desire to open a related hospice asset for patients needing that service. As our patients near the end of their lives, the best thing we can do for them is seamlessly transfer them into excellent hospice services. We saw a clear correlation between home health and hospice. A definite aligned opportunity. As we cleaned up our home health operations, paid down our debt, and generated incremental cash, we used the new funds to acquire and build hospice businesses in our markets. In a short period, we grew from the nation's 11th-largest hospice company to the third-largest. We discovered natural synergies operating home health and hospice business sectors together. We also created independent value for both sectors through their complementary activities.

We decided that providing a full continuum of home care required Amedisys to enter the personal care business. Personal care is unskilled (nonclinical) home care where aides assist patients with activities of daily living (ADLs). These activities include helping people ambulate (walk), bathe, go to the toilet, take their meds, eat properly, shop, and run errands. There is very strong evidence that losing the ability to do any of these things will accelerate sickness, injury, and entry into institutionalized care. Keeping patients on top of their ADLs keeps them in their homes and out of institutions.

Amedisys acquired personal care companies in Massachusetts, Tennessee, and Florida. We learned about the business. Successfully hiring and managing nonclinical aides has been difficult for us. The average wage for personal care workers is $15 to $20 per hour. The turnover is high, as much as 60 percent for us. The industry average can be close to 100 percent. It's a fundamentally different business than either home care or hospice. Consequently, we concluded that personal care wasn't a good fit as a new business line for Amedisys.

So instead of expanding into a sector where Amedisys didn't have any distinctive capabilities, we decided our best strategy was to contract with locally owned personal care companies and integrate their offerings into our clinical care platforms. That way our patients could receive the best mix of home-based care services. Our job is to combine it all together and coordinate it into a care plan that gives our patients the right services at the right time when they need them most.

Most recently, Amedisys acquired a hospital-at-home company called Contessa. Contessa provides home-based care at a much higher acuity level than the Amedisys home care platform. Contessa works with patients, hospitals, and insurers to give patients the option of hospital-level care in their homes.

Contessa replicates this model for nursing home care through its "SNF-at-home" program. Contessa also provides palliative care. Palliative care is generally the care level just before hospice. Unlike hospice care, palliative care takes care of declining patients but looks for curative treatments or care as well. By contrast, hospice only manages the comfort and pain of its patients as they move toward death.

On my visits to hospice care centers, center leaders invariably asked whether they could launch palliative care programs. It would allow them to transition people more precisely from home health. It would enable more intensive pain management without the finality of the decision for hospice care. As patients declined further, they could transition more easily into hospice care. Many patients referred to Amedisys for hospice care needed and would have preferred palliative care. Unfortunately, palliative programs are huge money losers. CMS does not adequately pay for palliative care services, so far too often patients don't receive the palliative care they deserve. It's tragic.

However, palliative care was the right thing to do for many patients, so Amedisys launched a palliative program. We lost lots of money, but we learned about this business and continued to work the problem. With Contessa, we solved the financial dilemma by offering risk-based palliative care. We approached managed care insurers (payers) and convinced them that we could manage this patient group better than they could. Early days, but so far we are doing a great job for our patients and demonstrating the economic viability of our palliative care model.

Over the course of my seven years as CEO, Amedisys expanded from one business offering to six, but they are all within the broader home care space. In a synergistic way, these six home care segments feed off and support one other. Each makes the others better. With each new home care segment, we become a more distinctive and holistic home care provider. The uniqueness of our service model drives Amedisys's value proposition and competitive market differentiation. In this way, Amedisys's service diversification has benefited shareholders as well as patients.

When I was running strategy for Humana, we built a one-page SOAP (strategy on a page) graphic that we called the "Horn of Plenty." It established value as Humana's core operating tenet and illustrated how our business and capabilities created value synergistically. The graphic arrayed Humana's businesses and capabilities in proximity to the company's core mission of value creation. This illustrated the core functions requiring enhancement as well as both proximate and ancillary functions. The greater the distance between a function and the core, the less Humana needed to own and control that function. Pictures can be worth a thousand words. By scanning this single page, our team knew whether to buy, build, partner, or contract to develop capabilities that supported our strategic vision (see Figure 6.2).

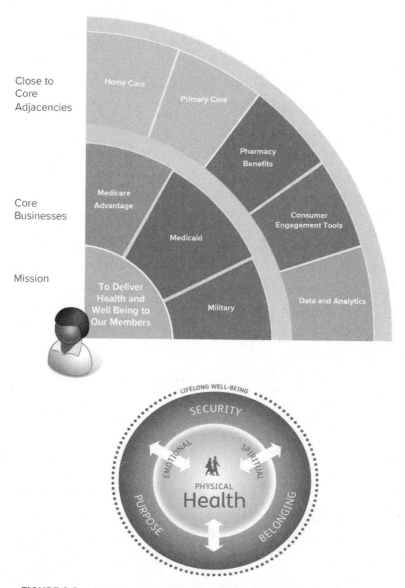

Close to
Core
Adjacencies

Core
Businesses

Mission

FIGURE 6.2 As illustrated by Humana's "Horn of Plenty," businesses grow from their core outward by serving the needs of customers.

Back to Amedisys. Our Golden Rule strategy became a virtuous circle where the component parts reinforced one another as the company grew. We started with the ambitious (and I would add right thing to do) goal to provide the best care possible for our patients. We realized that we needed to have the best employees to deliver that great care. We also knew that our great employees needed to have the best tools to create a conducive working environment where our employees could function at the highest performance levels. We also needed to have the best managers and leaders to nurture and sustain our employees. That's why we focused so intensely on reducing turnover.

I use the word "best" a lot in describing our strategy. The word "best," however, is useless without the ability to measure relative performance and outcomes. Best has to mean "better than the competition," but it requires metrics to validate that claim. We realized this and developed explicit measures and tools for defining, measuring, and tracking the company's "bestness."

As we executed our strategy, Amedisys rewarded its shareholders, those who bet their money and put their faith in the story. Our stock grew at a higher multiple than that of our competitors because we were doing the right thing better than they were.

Our Golden Rule strategy is simple in concept but difficult to execute. Treat your people well. They in turn will treat the customers well, and the company will prosper. The reason this strategy is better than most is because we have found ways to make it personal and moral. That took Amedisys into another dimension. It got us out of the profane and into the sacred. By creating a virtuous circle with the best caregivers, managers, tools, and working environment, we accomplished good by any and all measures. That is a unique thing in this world. Make a living by doing good. Make a positive difference in the world. Send out good vibes to whatever God is out there watching us.

Pursuing a Golden Rule strategy is a never-ending endeavor. At Amedisys, we took the first steps and achieved success. The company's table is set. In order to maintain our high performance level and continue our successful run, we must continue to treat one another and our patients as we would like others to treat us. We have been able to show that businesses and economics can coexist with morality and noble purpose. There are no shortcuts.

I believe the Amedisys culture can be self-sustaining and prosperous. After I leave, new leaders can push the company to even higher levels of performance and accomplishment if they never lose sight of the Golden Rule. Home is where the care is. Let us continue to find ways to make home-based care more effective and compassionate. My hope for Amedisys is that we individually and collectively will find ways to surprise ourselves by doing good work on behalf of our patients. Being the best in pursuit of this noble goal is a calling that we're privileged to share.

If we continue to have the evangelical belief that almost nothing we do in this life will be better than delivering great care, everything will be much better than fine. If we continue to put this vision in front of ourselves and work every day to make it real, our people will lead enlightened lives as they do much good in the world.

That's what we have done at Amedisys, and it is what I hope and pray the company will continue to do after I depart as CEO: Keep jumping into care of others with full faith. It's an elevated form of being that creates sacred space in the service of others in their homes.

Diving into great work without hesitation is joyful, soulful, enriching, and collective. It's ironic that the secret of leading a great life comes in service to others. We're at our best when we help others and let others help us.

KEY TAKEAWAYS

- At Amedisys, we position ourselves to be where the industry is moving. We exploit competitive advantages by continuously enhancing our service offerings.

- Healthcare services are moving into the home. That's Amedisys's sweet spot, but it won't last unless we extend our expertise and services further. It is important that we do that to help our main customer, Medicare, catch up to health systems in other advanced economies.

- The dilemma most businesses confront is preparing for the future (making the right bets) when the present is not the future but pays the bills. You have to do both. Balancing the old with the new.

- By narrowing our focus, we expanded our horizons. The deeper we dig into doing singular things well, the more we see promising opportunities emerge.

- Stay close to your core strengths. Appreciate where the company generates value. Build your own Horn of Plenty to grow outward from the core. This way the company will innovate in places, close to the core, where it has the highest probability of success.

7

STAGING
TRANSFORMATION

There are distinct stages along a company's transformation journey, particularly for organizations like Amedisys that have confronted an existential crisis. The stages move in sequence from turnaround to stability to growth to transformation. Each has unique attributes and requires specific skills and capabilities. This chapter dives into the turnaround stage. It's intense, immediate, and life-altering for the company and its CEO, so it deserves special attention. The next chapter addresses the subsequent stages.

Not many leaders are effective in all stages of a company's turnaround and repositioning. CEOs need to be aware of their company's relative progress within its metamorphosis and manage accordingly. That is neither easy nor for the faint of heart. As readers will observe, the theory and practice of organizational transformation came together for me at Amedisys.

TURNAROUND STAGE

My first stage at Amedisys, or as I like to refer to it "my first test," was a full-blown turnaround. The company was in crisis. Before I had become its CEO, the company's stock had sunk below $11 per share. When I joined the company, Amedisys had been leaderless for over six months. The CFO was serving as the interim CEO. The company was badly missing its financial projections. It had just paid a massive $150 million government fine with borrowed funds and agreed to a five-year probationary corporate integrity agreement.

Even worse, Amedisys was betting its future on a misguided vision of becoming a software company. We had hired several hundred people and invested tens of millions of dollars to create the new software platform (AMS3) to replace our existing home-built, cumbersome platform (AMS2). The company "starved" its core care businesses to fund the AMS3's development costs. When introduced, AMS3 confounded our care centers and wreaked havoc with operations. If AMS2 was Frankenstein, AMS3 was the son of Frankenstein!

We were rapidly losing employees. Working for Amedisys was a one-way street, "our way or the highway." Our clinical leaders could not agree on anything, so we operated without standardized clinical protocols. We could not define what constituted good service, so the company had no baseline for improving its performance. Amedisys was burning, and no one was putting out the fires.

I did my walkabout through field operations to gain strategic clarity. That journey led to a three-pronged strategy: (1) Deliver the best quality care; (2) hire and retain the best people; and (3) support our people with the best tools. Pretty simple, but Amedisys was doing none of this. In many situations, we were doing the opposite.

Getting our clinicians on the same page regarding quality standards/metrics was an immediate imperative. With our operations in a tailspin, clinicians were fighting over the quality equivalent of, "If a tree falls in the forest and no one hears it, does it make a sound?" It is impossible to deliver high-quality service without defining what quality is. This indecision was rippling through our workforce. Amedisys's clinician turnover rate, although average for the industry (bad spellers in a bad row), was very high (mid-40 percent range) and increasing. No company can deliver high-quality care with such accelerated turnover.

As I took the helm, Amedisys was going backward. We had unhappy investors, analysts, and partners. One large, activist shareholder was very unhappy with the company and my appointment as CEO. He called and told me I was the worst possible choice. Since he had no confidence in my ability to run the company, he urged me to seek a merger with one of our competitors. I have had much warmer welcomes.

In a turnaround, as everything is falling, the first thing a new CEO has to do is find out who on the management team wants to achieve stability by enacting meaningful change. There's no room for dissidents or debates or malingering delays. Those who remain must commit to the new vision, strategy, and teamwork required to achieve stability. No one intentionally gets up every morning and says, "I want to do the utmost damage to my company by pursuing the wrong agenda." Those advocating for policies and initiatives that were actually harming Amedisys didn't see it that way. They felt the existing strategic plan was right. It just needed a little more time and resources to prove its mettle. They were drinking their own bathwater and needed to leave the company.

As performance spiraled downward, a bunker mentality emerged inside the leadership team. Amedisys's senior executives began closing themselves and the company off from its customers and markets. They stopped listening and started preaching. Their solutions were beautiful narrations in the abstract but impractical and underwhelming in practice. Honesty was in short supply. Leadership wasn't acknowledging hard issues. It was lacking verifiable market intelligence. As a result, Amedisys lost its grounding and became untethered from its mission. As I stepped through the front door, getting our people to believe again in themselves and the company was my primary objective.

My foray into our markets was key to getting Amedisys's operations turned around. Getting honest, market-based feedback on what our care centers needed and wanted, as well as a clear understanding of how our services stacked up against those offered by our competitors, was essential for developing a workable turnaround plan. Armed with this critical information, we set our goals and packaged up what we needed to do into a few achievable initiatives. We worked backward from our goals to develop detailed to-do lists and work plans. These became the actions we needed to take to get us where we wanted to go. We enlisted all our people in building the new Amedisys. We repeated our narrative over and over again until it became real, achievable, and tangible.

We also monitored our performance closely, so we could adhere to our narrative and self-correct when we strayed. This required the company to develop analytics and tracking tools. We kept working at it until we could almost instantaneously monitor our progress in several crucial areas. If something started going off the rails, we knew about it quickly.

We also researched and modeled performance scenarios focusing on the three strategic prongs of quality, people, and tools. We used basic psychology to create positive momentum for change. We teed up some easy wins to instill confidence within the workforce. These were learning opportunities. We publicly overpraised those who achieved early wins, so the organization would clearly understand the paths to success in the new Amedisys.

Quality, people, and tools are categorically broad with multiple layers and component pieces below. We needed to leverage these layers and component pieces to achieve success and show results. Accordingly, we broke down each goal into bite-sized, doable tasks. We tracked success and built road maps for broader program development, so our employees would understand how small successes contributed to make a greater whole.

My belief after being involved in several turnarounds is that there has to be a leveling acknowledgment. The company has to collectively realize and admit that it was headed down the wrong path. This is hard. It makes the company leaders, who oversaw the failed strategy, vulnerable. There's always a desire to punish those responsible for guessing wrong and failing to see and/or act on the warning signs, but it is more complicated than that.

If leaders were uniformly hearing warning signs, no doubt they would adjust strategies and tactics. Often their loyalists lead them astray. As a consequence, leaders double down to justify their strategies. They seek confirming snippets of positive news and block out danger signs. They preach the need to remain stalwart, stay the course. They tell themselves and anyone who will listen to persevere, keep the faith, and eventually we'll get there. Unfortunately, more commitment to failed strategies leads to even more dismal operating results. As the center unravels, the organization spins out of control.

Most companies organize around execution, not examination. They believe that too much examination creates a muddle. There are many operational diehards who believe that consistent execution will get you to where you need to go 90 percent of the time. That may be right, but there are two key signs that a company is heading down the wrong path:

1. Operating successfully is getting harder, not easier. There are no breakthrough points in sight. Generally if you are heading in the right direction, you work hard to get to speed and then can pull back on the throttle. When you are heading down the wrong path, things just get harder and harder.

2. The organization's core functions and competitive advantages are deteriorating. The few things that the company and its people were put on this earth to do are getting worse, not better. The projects that should create stability and differentiation are not what the company is good at doing, so they aren't generating expected rewards.

When operations are spiraling downward, leaders need to seek "solid ground" and build on the company's strengths. Amedisys's core strength was delivering high-quality care to our patients. If we did that first, our people would follow, and we'd get better and better, and all the resultant benefits of delivering the best care would follow. At our nadir, we lost this vision completely. Amedisys had lost confidence that it could sustain itself by resuscitating the core business, so it was flailing away, tilting at windmills, hoping for a miracle. When I arrived, the organization was a diverse collection of "Hail Mary" attempts to pull victory from the jaws of defeat. That can happen, but it's rare. It certainly wasn't going to happen here.

My early visits to our care centers cemented my belief that high-quality care delivery was the essence of what we did. It was in our DNA. This was the essential thing the company was good at doing, what we were put on this earth to do. Amedisys served a vital societal need for compassionate, home-based care. The marketplace would reward us if we regained our confidence and reinvigorated our raison d'être. From that point on, we cut anything that did not support that mission. We moved out anyone who opposed this singular focus. We found our simple song and needed to bring our singers together to perform their parts in harmony with one another. This simple but elegant strategy, to focus like a laser beam on delivering high-quality care, empowered our people. It gave them clarity and purpose. It enabled them to sort through their individual muddles and make decisions that supported the company's greater good.

When a new leader walks into a situation that requires a turnaround, there are always profound voids due to a lack of balance, lack of stated direction, and/or a confusing strategy. The key is to reset the company's mantra in a way that excites employees about the company's new direction and its potential to reshape the marketplace. Our new mantra centered on caring for patients in their homes. It's where they want to be. We only get the privilege to provide that care if we do it well. To do it well, we need to have the best quality care delivered by the best people with the best tools.

A big problem with turnarounds is finding capable managers. Very few leaders choose to dive headlong into a dumpster fire. I was lucky to have several talented people with whom I'd worked who were willing to join me at Amedisys. Many were fringe employees at Humana whose careers had stalled due to no fault of their own. They did not want to continue stagnating in a corporate purgatory. Others included consultants between gigs and corporate professionals between jobs. They were a motley crew willing to try something different. Better-positioned professionals with the skills I needed were not interested or available. Our circumstances were too risky for them.

By most measures, I had assembled a ragtag team, but they were the right people at that time for the situation in which Amedisys found itself. They worked ruthlessly hard to help me right the ship. I paid them disproportionately in stock options because the company could not afford to pay high salaries. We were collectively taking a big financial risk, but the rewards would be substantial if we could turn the company around.

Baton Rouge as the only corporate headquarters was a problem. The complaint we always heard from professionals about relocating to Baton Rouge went something like this: "This is the only healthcare game in town. This is a turnaround. What happens if it doesn't work? I'm completely stuck." For me, Baton Rouge is a wonderful place with the best people you could ever know. Our staff does an excellent job, but the complete set of skills needed to catapult the company forward were almost impossible to find there.

I quickly established an executive headquarters in Nashville. KKR, Amedisys's lead investor, helped us vet other locations, but Nashville was the clear choice. In contrast to Baton Rouge, Nashville is a healthcare mecca. It's the industry's beating heart, and healthcare professionals want, even need, to be there.

There are over 500 healthcare companies in Nashville with local, national, and international reach. The region's healthcare ecosystem generates almost $100 billion in annual revenues globally and employs almost 600,000 workers. It was much easier to recruit the right people to work in Nashville and have them commute to Baton Rouge when needed. Many of the industry analysts also lived in Nashville, and our investors came through town several times a year. Having a Nashville presence for Amedisys was a proverbial no-brainer. Having a presence there would benefit the company enormously.

Despite its obvious logic, establishing a Nashville base stressed our employees in Baton Rouge. Many thought it was a first step toward moving the entire headquarters to Nashville. It turned out that having two locations, although sometimes difficult, put us at the center of the healthcare dialogue. We became a more visible member of the healthcare ecosystem and a more active participant in industry conversations while maintaining our legacy and core base of employees.

Our turnaround team was a diverse amalgamation of mercenaries but got the initial job done. It was not anyone's idea of an A-team, but people did an A+ job of getting us out of the ditch and stabilizing operations. They did what turnaround people are meant to do, find solid ground and build up from there. We executed on a few core strategies. The company fell into line. Once stabilized, Amedisys started to jerk and lurch toward becoming what it was meant to be.

The best example of this was in quality. As I stated previously, our clinicians couldn't decide what constituted high-quality home care. Hence, the company operated with no real quality standards. After debating this issue ad nauseam internally, I decided to let our customers define quality for us. Our biggest customer was the US government. As noted earlier in the book, Medicare employs a star rating system for home care providers. Amedisys was not a stellar "star" performer. Rather than debate Medicare on quality standards, we decided to adopt its star rating system as our benchmark. We started with a middling 3.4 average star rating out of a possible 5.0 stars. We needed to do better.

As we put all our efforts into becoming the best home care provider, the company's average star-rating score improved all the way up to 4.6. Multiple benefits accrue to organizations that achieve high star ratings. Referrals increase. Volume and revenues improve. Payment bonuses materialize. As a result, Amedisys's margins leapt upward.

We turned quality into both a science and a passion. We trained our clinicians on quality relentlessly. We tracked their performance and rewarded those who hit the marks. This pursuit of quality revealed our hidden and underemphasized strength in care delivery. As the organization rediscovered our innate abilities, they came forth powerfully in service to patients. It was wonderful to watch.

High-quality care delivery was the essential ingredient necessary for Amedisys to succeed. Focusing on quality paid enormous dividends. Turnover declined. Recruiting became easier. Productivity improved. Margins expanded. The company grew faster. By aligning around quality, we found our collective purpose. We winnowed out what was unimportant. We doubled down on what made us great.

While thrilling, turnarounds are life-sucking. They are highly stressful, chaotic, jarring, and physically demanding. As the CEO, I had to be on all the time and never got enough rest. The to-do lists are endless. Explosions are everywhere. Second-guessing decisions becomes a daily reality, particularly when the choices are bad, even torturous. Failure is always at the door. It's hard to get proper footing. Everyone is yelling and urgently giving advice, much of it ill-conceived. Worst of all, there is collateral damage. Necessary decisions hurt people. Sometimes badly and often through no fault of their own. That is the soul-wrenching part.

Tough decisions cannot be avoided. We had to sort through our personnel and identify those with enough belief and moxie to tough it out. There are numerous good people who can't get there. The sorting machine is dialed up to brutal. There isn't room for nuance in turnarounds. It gums things up. There can be no tolerance for equivocators or dissenters when a company is scraping bottom. Get on the ship and row in unison with us or get off. Everyone has to drink the Kool-Aid. Extreme clarity abounds and supports the tough decision-making. This can overwhelm smart and sensitive professionals not fully committed to the turnaround. Purity of direction and intent win. A company in turnaround mode can't brook doubt or ambiguity. The lines are clear and the colors are bright. The path to salvation is a straight line. Doubters, cynics, questioners, contemplative types are no good for a company beset with hard choices.

When it's over, some who were pushed out during the heat of battle will not like the company and its leaders, and may even revile them. Some may suffer career ruin. In the forced haste, leaders invariably make wrong decisions. When I can, I find and apologize to those my bad decisions affected. Sometimes they will accept my apology. Often they don't.

Turnarounds shock the system. They strip everything down to the basics and then rebuild. Unfortunately, the hard lessons learned during a turnaround are invariably forgotten as companies steady and move forward. The bare-bones operating intensity gets subsumed by a cushiness that creeps back into the system. If a company is not careful, tangential activities will bloat the company and initiate another decline. Business life is cyclical, and most companies ultimately die. Extreme focus is good, but only for a short while. If things settle down to a hard but measured pace, the company will be safe. Extremes on any front cause imbalance. That's when organizations lose control.

"A Good Man Is Hard to Find" by Flannery O'Connor is among the best short stories ever written. An elderly woman traveling with her family encounters an escaped prisoner and killer named The Misfit. Recognizing him creates a moment of awful clarity and certain death. As she realizes that her life has consisted of senseless platitudes based on false truths, The Misfit shoots her. Nothing focuses the mind like an execution. As she lies dying on the ground, The Misfit says to his companion, "She would of been a good woman, . . . if it had been someone there to shoot her every minute of her life."

That's what a good turnaround is, a revelation, someone shooting you every minute of your life. In all its starkness, there are moments of extreme clarity and unvarnished grace during the worst moments of a turnaround. Leaders must grab and build upon these insights. In retrospect, human nature often minimizes the turnaround's pain.

Once resettled, most companies forget the hard lessons and soften up. Some get back into trouble. The marketplace is unsentimental. Deliver value or disappear. The Misfit was right. To be good requires someone ready to put a bullet in the company the minute it lapses.

KEY TAKEAWAYS

- As companies transform, they pass through four very distinctive stages: turnaround, stability, growth, and transformation. Leaders have to recognize and honor the requirements of each stage in order to pass through it and onto the next one.
- Companies require different skills and capabilities within each stage. Often the people who got you here won't get you there. Respect the requirements of each stage as you construct strategies and teams. This is where the wonderful quality of loyalty can be counterproductive.
- Honor and reward the contributions of employees as they leave the company. Practice the Golden Rule.
- Turnarounds are the apex and nadir of human experience at the same time. They can restore organizations if they force honest evaluation and drive critical, hard choices. Honest evaluation in a crisis forces leaders to strip away preconceptions and pretenses. It reveals the basic truths of where and how things stand in the organization.
- Invariably, there are true kernels of value buried within the organization. Turnarounds force leaders to find solid ground on which to build the new, streamlined company. Without solid ground, no initiatives can stand.

- Go to the market and ask your customers what your company is and where it stands. This inquiry will reveal real strengths and real weaknesses. Customers hold the truest mirror. Build upon what the market values.
- For clarity, metaphorically "shoot yourself every day." In a turnaround, the revelations such honesty brings are liberating.

8

FROM STABILITY TO GROWTH AND BEYOND

The famous British writer Samuel Johnson astutely observed that "nothing so concentrates the mind as the sight of the gallows." Turnarounds represent life-or-death challenges for companies. They focus the corporate mind. Those companies that avoid execution live to fight another day. This chapter addresses the three subsequent stages—stability, growth, and transformation—that follow a turnaround. Each has unique attributes and challenges. It's important to execute each stage properly to avoid regressing and, god forbid, having to execute another turnaround.

STABILITY STAGE

After the "Sturm und Drang" of the turnaround, surviving companies segue into a period of stability. All of a sudden, leaders realize that the storm has passed. The company has lived to fight another day. There's time to take a deep breath, survey the scene, take stock of the damage, and assemble a rebuilding plan. Problems remain, but they are less urgent. Panic has subsided. Sprigs of hope poke through the wreckage. They become building blocks for new strategies and sources of near-term wins.

Then there is the team—the band of loyal mercenaries who fight alongside the CEO to staunch the bleeding and stabilize operations. These professionals are built for fighting. Most (but not all) adrenaline junkies, by nature, want to move on to the next impossible challenge. To a hammer, every problem looks like a nail. The primary characteristic of turnaround specialists is that they love a good fight. These are not peacetime citizens. Most cannot adapt to a stable operating environment.

Just as on a track team, companies need different types of runners for different stages of the race toward transformation. Sprinters can't win marathons. Once the war is over, the company no longer needs marauding bands of turnaround specialists wandering through the organization looking for fights. They create too much disruption. During the stability stage, a company's managers evolve into beat cops. They keep the peace and work to improve the hard-won ground conquered during the turnaround.

Even mercenaries have feelings. Some don't want to leave even when they know it's time. Fortunately, compensation for our turnaround specialists at Amedisys included very attractive stock options. We did not have sufficient cash to pay large salaries. With the company's improved performance and rising stock price, our turnaround experts earned millions of dollars cashing out Amedisys stock options. That made the parting easier.

At the same time, these individuals were my colleagues and friends. They were in the trenches with me and fought with everything they had to get Amedisys out of peril. Their efforts saved the company. Were they the most polished executives? Not even close. When a company like Amedisys is confronting a near-death experience, finding top executives is not an option. I quickly assembled the best team I could for the task at hand, but the group was a ragtag band of brothers and sisters. I called them and they came—free agents, consultants, people in flux, out-of-favor executives were what I could get. They were loyal. They gave their all. Yet it was time for them to move on. The company needed different skills for when it achieved stability.

Some got it; others didn't. The ones who didn't get it were the hardest to get to leave. They believed they'd earned the right to continue with Amedisys without altering their working orientations. Continued employment was their due, their privilege, their reward for loyal service. Some thought they could evolve with the organization. I gave them the chance, but most failed.

In business, good CEOs quickly learn that dispassion has to be the primary emotion in assembling, picking, and sorting a team. Great CEOs employ compassion when dealing with all people coming, going, and staying. We made it part of the Amedisys culture to celebrate our colleagues as they left the company by acknowledging them as people and for their accomplishments. The good news is that most of our departing professionals left with a pile of cash, discernible achievements, good references, and high praise from me. Almost all landed on their feet in environments more suited to their particular talents.

That's the hard truth of driving an organization through its evolutionary stages. Different evolutionary stages require different strategies, skills, and capabilities. The horses that pull a company through are its people. Professionals can evolve and operate at high performance levels in different stages, but most don't, and very few can change as quickly as required.

Performance assessments are never just about the individual; they're always about what's best for the company. The CEO is ultimately responsible for assembling and evaluating a company's leadership team. He or she needs a "cold eye" for keeping the company's talent and capabilities on pace and in sync with the company's needs. Exercising that cold-eye mentality is one of the hardest parts of being a CEO. That's why it can be lonely at the top.

The stability stage was pleasant for me, but it was a bit boring. Luckily, it was brief. It enabled all of us to recharge our engines before revving up for growth. The work undertaken during the stability stage encompasses contemplation, reflection, scenario running, and strategic planning. It also centers on improving the operational excellence of the company's core business functions.

At Amedisys, we had hacked and cut away the company's non-core functions and assets. We were betting Amedisys's future on operating the company's core functions superbly well. This required investment in new systems and infrastructure. Specifically, we hired a team to enhance our quality tracking and training capabilities. We built tools to identify and fix care centers with high turnover and deteriorating performance. We developed feedback loops, analytics, and tracking technologies. We incentivized and rewarded employees who produced great results. We removed care center leaders with consistently high turnover rates.

Teams of implementation experts helped roll out our new clinical software. We put huge resources into training our employees and tracking their use of the new software platform. We wanted to make sure they took full advantage of the clinical software's benefits. Follow-up teams assisted those struggling post-rollout. Software specialists drove better use of technologies into our care delivery methods. Frontline care delivery is Amedisys's core strength. Changing mechanics demanded a lot of attention. We had to get it right.

We focused on executing our core really well—we wrote and mapped out a plan, gauged our ambitions to make them tough but achievable, and put experts to work. We found people who really want to get the job done, gave them the resources required to get it done, cleared the decks of other distractions, got everyone aligned and excited, and rewarded excellence. Guess what happened? We got it done!

Our stabilization stage was nice and cozy. We were safe now. In a nice, protected harbor out of the chaotic storm on the wide, senseless ocean. We could repair our storm-damaged ship, focus on strengthening our core, and position ourselves for future growth.

Focusing solely on quality, people, and tools in our core home care business drove out all distractions. Amedisys rapidly started to generate strong organizational cash flow. The tools, prioritization, and workflow streamlining drove out wasted costs and eliminated redundancies. By becoming the highest-quality home care provider, volume at our care centers grew quickly. Optimizing our human capital by reducing turnover, creating efficiencies, using better technologies, and improving productivity generated higher performance margins. Amedisys's profitability kept getting better and better as we focused more and more on being the best place for our people to practice the art of caring.

During this time, I endeavored to tie everything together. I wanted to demonstrate the synergies embedded within Amedisys's component parts—how our initiatives correlated with and strengthened one another. For example, Amedisys's obsessive focus on quality engaged our caregivers, improved productivity, reduced turnover, and increased organizational cash flow. Quality made our caregivers want to wear the Amedisys uniform above all others. Quality ratings turbocharged growth. The 5-star care centers grew faster than the 4.5-star centers that grew faster than the 4-star centers and so on. Amedisys's focus on quality increased the demand for our care. Our multiple initiatives to improve quality correlated. They complemented and strengthened each other.

I specifically wanted to avoid acquisitions until Amedisys was strong and humming at its core operations. Acquisitions are disruptive. Regardless of their potential value, bringing new entities into a company's ecosphere triggers human and organizational turmoil. Leaders must prepare and be ready to address this inevitable turmoil when purchasing new assets.

At Amedisys, we did two very small deals first. I wanted to see how we accommodated new entities. We didn't do very well. The Amedisys diligence teams missed several important data points in their reviews. These dogs we bought were lovable but had fleas. Additionally, the integration of both new companies' assets into Amedisys's operations was difficult. Although they were small transactions, these first two deals proved to be excellent learning opportunities for future acquisitions, even if their lessons were painful and enduring. Over five years later, Amedisys is still addressing lingering issues from those initial acquisitions. Pick your mates well; a poor choice can irritate for a long time.

I was blunt with our board. We were 0 for 2 on our initial acquisitions. Fortunately, Amedisys generated an abundant amount of cash during this period. We eventually repaid all our debt, including acquisition-related debt. In fact, Amedisys was stockpiling enough cash that analysts, shareholders, and potential investors wanted to know how we were going to use it. We had to decide whether to make new investments or use the cash to enrich our shareholders through dividends and/or a stock buyback program. Doing the latter to me was embarrassing. If we did not know how to invest the money to generate accretive returns, then we weren't sufficiently opportunistic or forward-thinking. Not investing would send the wrong message to the marketplace. It was time to put our excess cash into use. It was time to grow.

GROWTH STAGE

So we had a nice period of stability. Amedisys focused, fixed, and righted its core home health business. Our new infrastructure positioned us well to increase market share. Unfortunately, getting the basics right wasn't going to be enough to grow and transform Amedisys into a more vibrant and much more valuable company. The problem was and still is that Medicare underfunds home care service provision. Relying solely on home care wouldn't take Amedisys to the promised land of turbocharged growth, a soaring stock price, and a robust market capitalization. We needed to do more.

For seven consecutive years, Medicare lowered its reimbursement rates for home care services. Additionally, CMS was in the midst of overhauling its payment models to reduce widespread fraud and abuse in the home health industry. If implemented, we estimated that the proposed changes would push half of all home care operators out of business. Here's the irony. It was the government's pricing system that triggered the fraudulent behaviors. The solution punished good and bad home care providers equally. Throwing out baby and bathwater come to mind?

Home health and hospice services are a very small part of Medicare's overall expenditures, about 7 percent. Yet, the home is where people want to receive treatments. Home-based care is less expensive, drives better outcomes, and has a much higher satisfaction rating than institutionalized nursing home care. The other OECD countries use home care much more widely than the United States. As a result, they generate better outcomes for lower costs. Access and use of home healthcare services to treat the chronically ill is far more efficient and effective than episodic acute interventions. Still, CMS keeps increasing reimbursement for hospital acute care treatments, the most expensive and least effective way to manage chronic conditions. Almost 80 percent of Medicare's total spend goes to hospitals and physicians each year with sizable year-over-year payment increases. Medicare's approach is illogical and misguided, but nonetheless a reality for Amedisys and other home care providers. We have overcome Medicare's payment cuts by becoming more efficient and effective operators. Good for Amedisys, but the rest of the home health industry is teetering.

Given these circumstances, I was still spending a week every month visiting our care centers. Wherever I went, I asked our home health leaders what they needed to grow their operations. Uniformly, they urged us to expand into hospice. There is a natural linkage between home care and hospice services. A large percentage of Amedisys's patients were eligible to receive Medicare-funded hospice services, but there weren't enough good places to refer them. Our care centers wanted to offer their clients seamless integration between home health and hospice services. Why not? Who wants more bureaucracy at the end of life?

Amedisys already had a small but very well-run hospice business. I hadn't paid much attention to it during the turnaround. Seemingly small, it was the 11th-largest hospice provider in the country but only generated a small percentage of the company's overall revenues. Unlike its payment for home care, Medicare was increasing payment for hospice care. That was interesting. The more we looked at hospice, the more sense it made to expand our hospice service offerings and integrate them into our care delivery platform.

Hospice, particularly in-home hospice, cares for patients in their last six months of life. Physicians must document the six-month-or-less expected life span for Medicare to reimburse hospice care services. They also must communicate this prognosis to the patients and their families. In turn, patients must waive access to curative care to initiate their hospice program. This last requirement is a big but necessary hurdle. Admitting certain death is difficult for most. Once under way, hospice care provides physical, mental, and spiritual comfort for the last months of life. It enables individuals to die on their own terms.

Hospice is a wonderful benefit. Most who experience and witness hospice care attest to and praise its attributes. The percentage of people selecting hospice has doubled in the past 15 years. Just over 50 percent of Americans now die under hospice care. Experts project hospice admissions will double again during the next seven years due to demographics and higher selection rates. This constitutes unprecedented growth for a well-established healthcare company. Hospice is especially popular with baby boomers, the majority of whom are now in their 60s and 70s. When their time comes, boomers overwhelmingly want to die at home in their own beds surrounded by family and friends.

A "planful" death is an illusion. Too many hospice patients believe they can stage-manage their final months, weeks, and days. Death comes in a myriad of ways that are not within our time frame or control. Sometimes, but not always, death comes peacefully to a conscious patient surrounded by loved ones. Despite the uncertainties, hospice guides people's deaths better than other alternatives, particularly medicalized death in a hospital connected to fluid tubes and monitors. By acknowledging their impending death, patients stop fighting the inevitable and focus instead on making the best use of their remaining time. A good death is a very powerful human experience for all involved. Ironically, patients on hospice care usually live longer than those with equivalent prognoses who continue to fight their disease and its inevitable outcome.

Hospice is a good business, but we have to operate it with soul. We must honor our moral obligations to our patients by always providing a level of pain relief and comfort that doesn't unduly compromise patients' cognitive functionality. Even though most dread it, death comes to us all. At Amedisys we view hospice care as a sacred responsibility. Great hospice care combines clinical pain management with counseling and spiritual support for the patients and their families at a low cost. It guides patients through life's final stage as humanely as possible.

Multiple research studies have concluded that the cost of a hospice death to Medicare is much less than that of a nonhospice death even though hospice patients live longer than those who die in hospitals while continuing to receive aggressive care. That's part of the reason that Medicare has increased funding for hospice services. As importantly, patients and their families increasingly prefer hospice care and give it high customer satisfaction scores. For Amedisys, the close linkages between home care and hospice spurred our desire to integrate the service platforms. The company was already in the hospice business and expert at performing it, reimbursement trends were good, and our care centers wanted to offer the service.

Beyond this, Amedisys needed to diversify. Home care is a vital business with a spectacular future but has suffered through a prolonged period of declining payment by governmental and commercial payers. As CEO, I wanted additional service offerings beyond home care to generate incremental revenues, reduce risk, and spur growth. With uncertainty clouding reimbursement for our core home care business and a pile of cash, Amedisys started an aggressive investment and acquisition program to grow its hospice business.

We went all in. Amedisys bought four hospice companies; two large and two medium-sized. We created a hospice development team that oversaw the siting and construction of brand-new hospice facilities. In two short years, Amedisys became the nation's third-largest hospice company.

Our timing was good. It was a buyer's market. The valuations at which we bought these four companies were attractive and accretive to Amedisys's operating portfolio. We were early buyers in what would turn into a very hot market. A year later, competitors following us into the hospice business were paying up to twice as much per hospice bed.

As always, the key to buying an asset successfully is knowing what its value will be a year or two later after its acquisition. When the honeymoon is over, the hard work of integration begins. Acquisitions force important strategic decisions that shape how the acquired company will operate within its new company, when the asset really gets tested, and when the inevitable shakeout begins.

These decisions affect the acquired company's people. That's important because they constitute most of the purchased company's acquired value. Service companies, especially in home-based care, have few hard assets. Purchasers, like Amedisys, are buying clinicians, business relationships, market presence, expertise, and possibly a good local brand. All ephemeral, and hence, vulnerable to flight.

As I mentioned earlier, we learned what not to do in the two small acquisitions Amedisys made during its stability stage. I had completed over 70 deals as head of mergers and acquisitions (M&A) and venture investment at Tenet and Humana. I also ran my own venture investment fund. That experience has given me a good idea about what does and does not preserve the value of acquired assets.

The first rule is to assume nothing. After the purchase, get flexible, because changes occur every day. Surprises happen constantly as the new business fully reveals itself. The acquisition process mimics an arranged marriage. The bride and groom only really get to know each other after the wedding. It's the same with buyers and sellers, except that the parties are not equal. Buyers are in control, so they have to figure out what to do with the constant flow of new information.

The second rule is that the purchaser has a year to resell—yes resell—its vision of future success to the acquired company's leaders. Get them on board with the new vision, or they will leave after their noncompete periods end. Worst case is that they take their sales proceeds and invest in a competitor or build something better to compete against the purchasing company. Often their people will follow them across the street to join competing companies.

Third, create a "gets list." It's imperative. A gets list details what each side expects to get from the transaction. There should be alignment between the parties right from the start. Sit down before the deal closes and agree in writing on each side's expectations for the executed transaction—buyer and seller. As a purchaser, be confident the company can deliver its part of the gets list. Don't sign up for anything your company can't do. That provides the moral high ground to hold the sellers to their promises to transfer all the potential value of the acquired assets.

Fourth, look at all the people who have just made "screw-you money" and imagine the company without them. More than likely, they'll leave after their noncompete period ends and/or their incentives vest. It won't just be money that drives them away. They'll explode over the ridiculous corporate contortions the purchaser forces upon them—linking up their technical systems, integrating payroll, merging back offices, and seeing several of their colleagues depart. Up-and-coming leaders who helped build the company but didn't make the huge bucks when their company sold usually determine if the purchased company has value. Make it worth their while to stay by moving them into the vacated leadership slots. Let these new leaders finally show what they can do and reward them for it.

Interestingly, de novos (Latin for "from the beginning or anew"), or new, investments are the safest way to grow volume and revenues. By starting from scratch within Amedisys, we found we could grow and build new programs and services most effectively. The challenges with de novo investments are time and accounting. First, de novos take longer to get up and running, but the company gets to plan and build its own structure, not inherit a flawed and/or unfamiliar one. Second, accounting rules work against de novos. The company cannot use prearranged bank loans to fund the investment like it can with acquisitions. Funding comes straight out of the company's operational cash flows, which negatively impacts earnings. Reducing income for new investments is a big disincentive for public companies that have to show progressive earnings growth.

Let me vent for a second. Accounting rules limit the most assured, safest, and most risk-free way for companies to grow. When purchasers, like Amedisys, acquire assets, they usually do so with debt financing from banking syndicates. Lenders evaluate potential acquisitions based on their projected post-acquisition EBITDA or cash flow. By borrowing, companies use debt on which they pay interest. That interest cost is not included in the EBITDA/cash flow figure. Eliminating the interest expense from EBITDA allows companies to sustain higher valuations. Consequently, it is relatively more cost effective to fund acquired assets from debt than to fund them from scratch with company cash. Why this has to be the case, why the incentives are so lopsided in favor of buying over building, still confuses me.

Back to Amedisys. After the turnaround, the company was operating its core home care business better and generating incremental profits and cash flow by doing so. Up to this point in the turnaround, we had avoided making acquisitions. Now operating a successful home care business and flush with cash, Amedisys was well positioned to acquire complementary assets, particularly since the home care industry was facing potentially huge payment cuts by Medicare for its services. Our strategy was to wait for this catastrophic event to happen and cheaply acquire distressed home care providers.

By pursuing this strategy, Amedisys could expand its footprint and generate coverage across the country, potentially becoming America's largest home care provider with a national footprint. We reasoned that this strategy would put us in a good position with fast-growing Medicare Advantage (MA) plans that required post-acute services, including home care, for their members. Our goal was to create a one-stop shop, an "easy button," for MA plans to contract with Amedisys. It's a great strategy, but we're still waiting to execute on it fully. Smaller and less profitable home care providers are barely functioning. Luckily, Amedisys now has a great hospice business to offset the declining reimbursement payments facing its home care business. The company is using its robust consolidated cash flow to build an acquisition war chest big enough to buy ailing home care assets should the promised Armageddon come.

Medicare's reimbursement system for home care services has been poorly designed from the outset. In the early 2000s, Medicare implemented a payment system that funds 60 percent of the home care services before they are actually delivered. In doing this, Medicare unwittingly became a bank for entrepreneurs to get into the home health business with very little up-front cash. Hence, the industry that Medicare funding helped create is now very crowded with small players. It is hard to manage and regulate. It is also riddled with fraud. Bad actors will establish a home care business, buy fake Medicare numbers, send out the first bills, collect the up-front payment, and skip town before the government catches on.

During Amedisys's growth stage, Medicare has tried to extricate itself from the mess its prepay system has created. Medicare's goal was to dramatically reduce up-front payments, eliminate fraud, incent industry consolidation, and manage fewer but much larger home care providers. Lobbying has prevented the huge catastrophic reimbursement cuts that Medicare envisioned. That's the good news. The bad news is that the accumulated small cuts in home care reimbursement over the last several years have cut service payments in aggregate by almost 17 percent. So Amedisys and other home care providers are presently languishing in a middle world of small continual cuts. We're enduring and preparing to get lucky.

During my walkabout and subsequent field visit, I learned about the importance of nonclinical care in the home. Nonclinical caregivers help our patients with activities of daily living (ADLs). Doing ADLs well enhances our clinical care service provision and drives superior results. ADLs, as you recall, involve helping patients with shopping, transportation, food preparation, bathing, toileting, ambulation (walking), and medications. When patients lose their ability to do these basic things, they become candidates for institutionalized care. At Amedisys, we want to prevent or delay transferring our patients into nursing homes for as long as possible.

Based on my observations of hundreds, if not thousands, of home visits, it's clear that our patients receive the best home-based care when they receive both clinical care and nonclinical personal care to address ADLs. With this understanding, Amedisys acquired the leading personal care company in Massachusetts along with several other Massachusetts-based providers to become the largest personal care company in the state. We also made some small acquisitions of personal care companies in Florida and Tennessee.

The personal care business is much different from our home care business. As an industry, personal care is even more fragmented than home care. Its caregivers are nonclinical professionals who receive much lower salaries than nurses. The turnover rates in the personal care industry range between 60 percent and over 100 percent. Much of the work is out-of-pocket, private-duty care for patients and families who can afford it. Medicaid funds personal care for low-income patients largely through PACE (Program for All-Inclusive Care for the Elderly), dually eligibles (those who receive both Medicare and Medicaid), and severely challenged patient groups. These patients often have multiple disabilities as well as behavioral health challenges. They often require near or full-time care.

Amedisys discovered it was not good at running its personal care businesses. From a skills and capabilities perspective, personal care wasn't a good fit with our home care and hospice services. Personal care businesses are often unstable. Keeping them intact is difficult with the constant turnover. After our initial investments, Amedisys deliberately kept its personal care business small and then sold it. Our present strategy is to build networks of preferred personal care business providers, learn from these business partners, and apply acquired knowledge to enhance our platforms for profitably delivering comprehensive home-based care services.

Instead of owning all home-based care businesses, our current strategy is to build large care networks through partnerships, like payers do, where we can deliver both personal and traditional home care services. To accomplish this, Amedisys partners with the best personal care agencies and integrates their care services into our platform. In this way, skilled clinical care and nonskilled personal care professionals work together on ADLs and social determinants of health. It's still early days. There have been lots of bumps in the road, many starts and stops, but the integrated strategy makes sense. The market wants the joint service provision but isn't paying for it yet. We'll see . . .

During our growth stage, Amedisys grew its core home care business organically by becoming the best in the industry at providing quality. Our industry-leading quality scores led to increased referrals, which turbocharged volume growth and bonus payments, which in turn increased margins and cash flow. We became the industry's best provider of home-based care services by focusing on our caregivers.

Golden Rule logic applies. It's impossible to deliver great care without great clinicians. Amedisys decreased clinician turnover and rewarded those who delivered quality results. We improved their tools so they could be their most effective and productive. Throughout, we were intent on making all of our company part of the care process. As Amedisys grew, it acquired and bulked up on a complementary business line, hospice. Hospice involves less complex care and execution and operates within an easier regulatory environment. It's been a great fit for us, and its economics are fantastic.

This strategic vision and the performance that accompanied it drove Amedisys's market capitalization (value) and stock price to unprecedented levels. The key to sustaining a high stock price is to grow the company's EBITDA (cash flow) as the best performer within a highly attractive industry. Investors often look at the ratio between a company's stock price and its EBITDA. That ratio is called the EBITDA "multiple." Higher is better. Amedisys's EBITDA multiple during my time as CEO jumped from 7x to more than 20x. That means for every dollar of cash flow, the company's relative value increased by 3x or more. Our profit margins also skyrocketed.

At this point we felt we were the best in the industry at our core home care and hospice businesses. But like all forward-thinking companies, we knew that our core businesses would mature and that new business models could emerge to displace us. So as the S-curve model of market dynamics depicts, companies should never take their foot off the gas. While basking in the success of the current business, companies must test, build, and/or buy the capabilities and assets required to remain competitive. This requires a perspective on the future and adapting to it. That's the next stage, transformation.

TRANSFORMATION STAGE

It's no secret that the healthcare industry is experiencing major disruption. Many incumbents are struggling to pivot into value-based care delivery while operating fee-for-service business models. Many, perhaps most, won't survive the transition intact. Before I left Amedisys, I wanted to plant some seeds that could sprout and position the company to compete effectively under value-based payment models.

My experience in the field revealed that payers, particularly large, vertically integrated payers like United Healthcare Group and CVS, are becoming increasingly dominant. They are generating huge profits, particularly in Medicare Advantage (MA) plans, and diversifying their revenue streams. They're profitable in MA because their plans offer more benefits to enrollees at a lower cost than traditional Medicare. To be profitable in MA, health plans have to acquire members and manage their health at a cost lower than a fixed, risk-adjusted monthly payment from Medicare. Given MA's current payment dynamics, it's not hard for commercial health insurers to offer plans to eligible consumers that are more attractive than traditional Medicare's fee-for-service plan. Traditional Medicare requires higher monthly premiums, copays, and deductibles and more limited services than most MA plans.

Traditional Medicare is an anachronistic, uncoordinated, unintegrated pay-by-the-drink program. Medicare Advantage has developed better plans by building value-based programs with narrower networks of providers and then making those providers accountable for the care they deliver.

MA is experiencing tremendous growth and now represents almost half of all Medicare enrollees. For Amedisys to thrive in the future, we will have to participate in value-based care delivery by taking financial risk for the services we provide to our patients. In essence, we will become responsible financially for the care we deliver and the outcome our care produces. This will require us to bet that we can manage our patients' care cost effectively while delivering superior care outcomes. This makes sense for our patients and American society. It is the right thing to do.

Also, it is very clear that healthcare services are migrating away from institutional settings due to their high cost, inconsistent quality, and inconvenience. The growing predominance of chronic diseases, which require proactive monitoring and care management, influences this trend. Also, COVID wreaked havoc with institutionalized care through high infection and death rates. In response, patients who could have stayed away from hospitals, nursing homes, and other institutionalized care settings, did.

Concurrently, interest in home-based care is increasing. New technologies that can monitor patients remotely and telemedicine tools that can allow clinicians to check in remotely on patients are enabling more home-based care delivery. As a consequence, home-based care is becoming more comprehensive and intensive. It is also generating superior outcomes relative to equivalent institutionalized care and with higher customer satisfaction.

All of this means that companies like Amedisys can and will deliver more and more complex care in the home. Payers want it, patients want it, and nonhospital providers (like Amedisys) want it. The hospital-centric care model is giving way to outpatient, ambulatory, and home care. With these powerful macro trends reshaping the healthcare marketplace, I wanted Amedisys to be the leader in pushing more care into the home and giving patients alternatives to institutionalized care.

There are a number of startup and early-stage companies that provide specialized and/or higher-acuity care in the home. We're running pilot programs with many of them to test their effectiveness. One startup that interested me was a small company named Clinically Home. Amedisys initially invested in Clinically Home, and then bought and ultimately mothballed it.

Clinically Home was a pioneer in providing hospital-level care in the home. Hospital-at-home care is not for all acute care patients, but it is just as or even more effective and always much less expensive for many patients. Clinically Home made some early progress prior to my time as CEO but was faltering when I came on board. We shelved it during the turnaround stage to focus on more urgent concerns. My intent was to revisit the concept once Amedisys recovered.

Positive market reactions for Clinically Home's services made me think, "There was a pony in there someplace." Payers in particular saw the cost and quality advantages of diverting people from hospitals into the home for certain acute conditions. Their clinical experts well understood the clinical, cost, and member preference advantages of hospital-at-home care.

One thing that happens with fast-growth companies, like Amedisys had become, is that new competitors enter the market and often offer differentiating services to steal market share. In essence, these new competitors are building market solutions for a not-too-distant future. For a host of reasons, incumbents are usually slow to respond to disruptive market trends. They know that the market is changing and that some of these "ankle biters" will become formidable and potentially superior competitors, but institutional inertia dilutes incumbents' ability to respond quickly. This happens even when customers demand the new services. Often incumbents succumb to the market pressure as upstart companies pass them by.

This is a hard position to be in, especially for a public company like Amedisys. We were at the peak of our growth. Our shareholders expected us to dominate our market and maximize profits from our core businesses. In reality, like all leading companies in dynamic markets, Amedisys also needed to be investing and building for the future. Siphoning capital for the future denigrates margins and reduces price-earnings multiples. It can become problematic with investors to acquire futuristic companies that can help incumbents succeed in a disrupting marketplace. Investors aren't always sympathetic. They want their returns now.

So what did Amedisys do? We saw the future and bought Contessa, the promising hospital-at-home company that I described in Chapter 6. Now we are pushing, pulling, and prodding the market to accept the future by expanding Contessa's service footprint. Through Contessa, patients who normally would require hospitalization can receive equivalent care in their homes. Contessa greatly expands Amedisys's service provision and revenue potential (see Figure 8.1).

Contessa partners with health systems. Its brilliantly constructed economic model allows hospitals to make more money on hospital-at-home patients than those admitted to its hospitals for equivalent treatments. That's how much more efficient Contessa's hospital-level care in the home is relative to traditional hospital care. The payers also get a significant discount for equal or better outcomes from hospital-at-home care. Patients get to stay out of the hospital and receive care in the comfort of their own homes. All constituencies get something out of it. Beautifully constructed, Contessa and companies like it will dominate in a decentralizing healthcare landscape. Accordingly, expect Contessa to be a big part of Amedisys's future.

The same logic applies to Contessa's SNF-at-home program. Close to 25 percent of COVID deaths (over 200,000 people) occurred in SNFs. Contessa delivers nursing-home-level care in people's homes for less cost with higher customer satisfaction rates and better outcomes. Treating frail patients in institutions carries higher infection and isolation risks that can magnify disease spread and

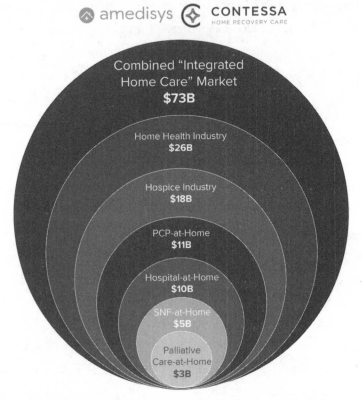

FIGURE 8.1   Contessa's incremental capabilities, particularly its hospital-at-home business, amplify Amedisys's ability to capture a larger share of the integrated home care market.

death. Contessa lowers these risks. It delivers better skilled nursing care at less cost in the home than occurs in institutions.

Palliative care provides another future market opportunity for Amedisys. As I discussed in Chapter 6, palliative care is a very important predecessor to hospice. Current Medicare payment policies make palliative care a money loser. Under the current reimbursement system, the only way palliative care can be effectively utilized is when MA plans pay for it in advance of sending members into hospice care. Medicare covers the costs of hospice care.

The sooner an MA plan can transition its members into hospice, the sooner it can transfer the cost of that dying member to the government. It is important to realize the last six months of life account for over 30 percent of Medicare total costs. A sizeable percentage of these costs result from unnecessary and heroic last-ditch efforts to prolong life. These efforts are not only costly; they often harm patients and accelerate death. Harshly stated but true. By contrast, home hospice is much more humane. With the support of their families, patients want to spend their final days at home. They accept the reality of their impending death and seek to die with dignity on their own terms.

Beyond hospital-at-home care, SNF-at-home care, and palliative care, nurse-driven primary care in the home for complex, chronically ill patients is another potential market opportunity for Amedisys. It's on our drafting board but not yet in the field. There is very strong demand for care management services among Medicare Advantage plans. Many MA plans currently delegate the care for their complex patients to physician groups that can keep these patients healthy and out of institutions. The demand for these types of care management services is much greater than the supply of physician groups available to them.

The answer to this supply-demand imbalance is very clear. Nurses, specifically nurse practitioners (NPs), have the necessary skills required to care for chronically complex patients. There are presently 211,000 nurse practitioners in the United States. They are exceptional caregivers who can deliver in the home almost all the chronic disease care services now provided by physician groups. At present, NPs conduct over a billion patient visits per year. The Bureau of Labor Statistics (BLS) projects that NPs will be the nation's fastest-growing profession over the next decade. The BLS expects the number of NPs in the United States to grow 45 percent by 2031.

As care migrates out of acute settings, care also will migrate to nonphysicians. This is both appropriate and necessary. Nurse practitioners are the most likely first stop in the eventual movement to transition care for chronically ill patients outside of institutions. Initially, NPs will work with physicians to "extend" their reach. For this reason, this category of NPs are often categorized as "extenders." Inevitably, NPs will manage their own patient panels. At Amedisys, we believe this approach will generate superior results. In some progressive markets, such as Minneapolis and Los Angeles, this is already occurring.

A recent McKinsey study projects that up to a quarter of all Medicare spending, more than double the 2022 expenditure level, could occur in the home by 2025. Amedisys agrees and expects to lead the charge. Market innovations, like those discussed above, will expand our service universe and give us the ability to provide better and more diverse care in the home to larger groups of patients. It will separate us from the pack. Our core home care business will generate sufficient cash to fund innovative Contessa-like service lines until they can stand on their own. As the market sees the value of what we are offering and as the proof points get put on the scoreboard, there will be an expansion and a migration of services to our new innovative services as they successfully test and validate themselves.

That's the theory and the dream. We're working manically to make sure our dream becomes reality. In the process, we will learn, fail, adjust, and try again. We will iterate until we develop programs that work. That is the nature of innovation and growth. As always, our customers, partners, and the market itself will stress-test our programs. If we pay attention to market signals, they will guide us to the right resource allocation decisions.

Transformative work is fun, new, and challenging. It also can be dangerous to profitability and status quo operations. It requires a tolerance for risk and failure that doesn't exist in most established businesses. There are clear demarcations between those who forge their way into the future and those who don't. Having both armies within the same organization creates potentially explosive competition for scarce resources. Managing transformation requires inspired leadership that can accommodate diversity of thought and action without the company becoming a festering Tower of Babel. Many aspire. Most fail. Those that do it right succeed beyond all expectations.

I am not a "burn-your-boats-at-the-shore, all-or-nothing" leader. The core informs and feeds the future. Its DNA is omnipresent as we migrate into our future selves. It is the safest way to drive transformation.

Like the creation myths, new worlds emerge from bodies of the old order. The best example is the Babylonian myth of the sky god Marduk. He kills his grandmother Tiamat and uses her body to form the earth and sky. Transformation is disruptive, sometimes violent, and often jarring, but it is also necessary. Adapt or die. Respond to market needs, or invariably you and your company will be left behind as others move forward.

Amedisys is making its strategic bets with Contessa and other initiatives to make sure it continues to grow and create more in-home capabilities. If we keep doing that, I'm convinced that the company will thrive. Transformation requires significant energy, compromises, and diplomacy to meet the market's constantly evolving demand. Heed the signals, iterate, and move forward!

One of the dangers of moving through the four stages of transformation at warp speed is that leaders miss learnings that they should have absorbed at each stage. Remember Winston Churchill's admonition, "Those that fail to learn from history are doomed to repeat it." Leaders never want to go backward, nor should they hastily build their companies' futures on a shaky, unvetted base.

At Amedisys we have learned to become honest listeners as the company has evolved. We constantly are trying to become what the market wants us to be. We understand we aren't always perfect and self-correct when we find ourselves heading down a wrong path. We have built a culture where mistakes are not a blight on managers' careers. This allows us to learn quickly, adapt, and move forward. We'll see how Amedisys does in the long run. My sense is we're giving it our open and honest best effort. If some initiatives come back to bite us, I imagine they'll be nips, not shark attacks. That will be the case as long as we keep listening, iterating, and doing our absolute best for our customers.

KEY TAKEAWAYS

- After the turnaround, take stock, reevaluate, and readjust the company's goals and priorities for an era of stability. This might require dismissing the warriors who executed the turnaround and welcoming new players with different skills.
- The stability stage allowed Amedisys to reaffirm its strategic priorities, develop an implementable strategy, and hardwire and build performance tracking tools and analytics.
- With more breathing space, the company can try new things on a small scale and fail without danger. Experimentation creates unforeseen opportunities, and failure teaches important lessons. Both are important to a company's future.
- Growth is addictive and often breeds hubris. It's important to attend to the company's core markets when it's doing well. Real-time market feedback keeps companies grounded and honest.

- To stabilize a company, it is important to diversify narrowly and safely. Add a line of business that is close to and aligns with the core. Understand that introducing new and unfamiliar businesses into our well-honed ecosystem is risky. Amedisys first expanded into a new services line (hospice) that our frontline managers wanted and where we had some experience. By staying close to the core, we were able to diversify safely.

- Acquisitions and deals are risky. Bringing in new cultures, practices, and people can be disruptive. Have realistic expectations. Being a conqueror rarely works. Treat acquired companies as new members of the family. Listen and learn. Overcommunicate.

- When integrating acquisitions, expect cultural dissonance and prepare for it.

- When an acquisition does not deliver as expected or it doesn't sync with your organization's expectations, pivot (as Amedisys is doing in personal care). When companies lack expertise and/or capabilities, build networks with aligned partners to implement strategic priorities. Partnering or building a new product or service offering is often a better alternative to acquisitions because it avoids the integration challenges.

- In a changing environment, transformation is essential for companies to survive and thrive. Move with the markets or become irrelevant. Amedisys bought an innovative company, Contessa, to amplify the strength of the company's home-based care platform. The Contessa acquisition illustrates the power of S-curve strategies to leverage the core to build for the future.

9

LOOKING BACK, LOOKING FORWARD

Among my favorite book quotations that I save and look at regularly are the last two lines from *The Adventures of Huckleberry Finn* by Mark Twain. Here they are:

> But I reckon I got to light out for the Territory ahead of the rest, because Aunt Sally she's going to adopt me and sivilize me, and I can't stand it. I been there before.

Rather than conform and become "sivilized," Huck decides to head west to "Indian Territory," where he can live independently and freely. Huck Finn changed everything in children's literature. Ernest Hemingway described *Huckleberry Finn* as the first real American novel. It was among the first to use regional vernacular and broke new literary ground in a myriad of ways. Twain captures the restless and wild spirit that drove America west. That spirit is still with us today.

I like the concept of "territory ahead." It appeals to the "seeker" in me, willing to venture out into the wild parts of the world and see what might happen. It represents a dreamy place of possibilities and the opportunity to tackle them head-on. A short synopsis of my idiosyncratic career reinforces that I am always seeking the "territory ahead."

I've been in healthcare for almost 25 years, although I became a healthcare lifer by accident. Despite being the son of a doctor and nurse, I had absolutely no interest in either medicine or healthcare. I was not great at science or math, so following in my parents' footsteps did not seem like a possibility. After my consulting work at McKinsey, I jumped into publishing with a focus on travel, adventure books, and magazines. I even jumped into cartography (mapmaking). I caught the travel bug at *National Geographic*, then got involved with canoe and kayak manufacturing, then tried and failed to buy a company that published adventure guidebooks.

I moved to Santa Barbara and needed to find a job. For a year, I commuted to Los Angeles for a gig, sponsored by the Getty Trust. Getty was trying to turn around a broken cultural museum. After that, I finally landed a job in Santa Barbara and no longer had to do that deadly LA commute. It happened to be at Tenet Healthcare, the only company in town that could use my skills as a strategist and deal guy. That's the random job that launched me into a perpetual healthcare professional.

Seven years at Tenet gave me the opportunity to understand the healthcare business and ecosystem. Running strategy and venture investments for Tenet, I learned how hospitals and physician practices worked. I also learned about other areas of healthcare and made some bets on futuristic plays for the healthcare marketplace—in technology, services outside of hospitals, and consumerism.

While at Tenet I also helped start several companies. They included a healthcare supply chain company called Broadlane, a nurse and clinical staffing company, an AI and database company that predicted patients' future healthcare needs, and an online clinical learning platform for nurses.

From Tenet, I went to help Broadlane grow new businesses that used our sourcing methodologies beyond the traditional materials-management functions. I then worked at Advisory Board helping it source deals in hospital labor management and analytics. I moved to New Zealand for a year and worked with a government-sponsored venture fund that invested in rural healthcare, telecom, and nutraceutical disciplines. I came back to the United States and worked with a small Chicago-based investment bank to launch a venture fund focused on technology-enabled healthcare service companies.

From there, I went to Humana and learned about the health insurance sector. I ran strategy, ventures, M&A, and innovations for Humana. We bought and integrated 40+ companies to push Humana forward into new territory. I learned how to use data and build clinical pathways, and I learned the ways in which value-based care did and didn't work. I learned how to design outcomes-based risk programs even as I struggled to understand underwriting and actuarial sciences. I became a huge proponent of incorporating behavioral health into benefit design as well as a strong advocate for consumerism in healthcare. I applied my marketing skills widely across the broad spectrum of healthcare services companies.

I then left Humana to help start a company, Alignment Healthcare, that managed the care of seniors with complex medical conditions. Finally, I joined Amedisys, where I became enamored by the potential for home-based care.

This resuscitation of my peripatetic career progress is not meant to impress. It shows that I never stayed long in jobs, no matter what the industry sector nor job responsibilities. At the same time, I have had the rather unique privilege of working within multiple sectors of the healthcare industry's massive ecosystem. My aperture is wide and constantly in search for the "territories ahead."

Until I arrived on the doorstep of Amedisys, my roles within the various companies and sectors where I'd worked were rather similar and focused on strategy. I'd try to figure out where the puck was going and then apply that perspective to investments and acquisitions—investing in and buying futuristic companies; partnering with companies that would prod us forward; finding hidden innovation buried inside mothballed enterprises; integrating new ideas to accelerate innovation and growth. My constant role was asking what the future is going to be and trying to move my companies toward that future proactively.

In one way or another, almost all my bosses' questions and admonitions were eerily similar: "What have we got?" "Are we missing anything?" "How long is this business going to last?" "Make sure we don't get surprised." "Make sure we don't get left behind."

Along the course of my career, I discovered I had a unique skill not much seen in the corporate world. I call it the "Picasso in the attic" eye. Roughly translated, it's the ability to find diamonds in the rough or see possibilities where others didn't. As a strategist, I would poke around and sort through my company's various assets and business processes—going into the metaphorical basements, closets, garages, and attics to see what we might have of value. I was allowed to question things freely, and often I found assets that the company had ignored or overlooked. These assets usually didn't fit cleanly into operations but had untapped potential if reconsidered and/or recast. One of my colleagues dubbed me the "King of the Island of Misfit Toys." It was an apt label. I was always pulling out buried products and ideas, wanting to know what could be done with them.

I liked to refer to this internal sleuthing for value as "intrapreneurism." Trying to create entrepreneurial opportunities within the company with assets that were already there. At Amedisys and other companies, my belief was and is that all the answers to all the key questions lie within the companies themselves. Leaders just need to look and listen really hard to find them. There is religious precedent for this belief. As the Roman philosopher Cicero observed, "Next to God we are nothing. To God we are everything." Most religions I've studied maintain there are pieces of God in all of us and everything around us. We just have to look hard to find those precious pieces.

Throughout my career, more than not, I was the guy the company expected to vet potential acquisitions and new ideas. I got to hear all the pitches. My job was to judge, "Is this something we should be interested in?" "Would this make us better at what we were doing? Did it propose a new opportunity for us to pursue that we had not seen or considered before? Was there value in something that would be meaningful later? Should we risk the inevitable disruption of bringing these entrepreneurs in to help us transform ourselves into a better company?"

Internal colleagues as well as external representatives sent me ideas and opportunities they thought our company should consider and exploit. Most corporate leaders are averse to rocking the boat with disruptive ideas and products. I had to be confident that an asset had real potential before promoting it to broader inspection and review.

Over time, I developed and refined a vetting process for new ideas, concepts, products, and companies. I would assemble an internal deal committee made up of frontline operators within the company. Ultimately, these were the managers who would breathe life into any new idea. Ideas that lacked their support were DOA. So I took any and all new companies, ideas, ventures, and partnership opportunities through a rigorous review process with these operators. They provided input and perspective and had ultimate decision authority.

In particular, we always invited those who would be directly affected by these new opportunities and would be responsible for their implementation. Twenty times to one, they killed the ideas I brought before them. I always respected their decisions. It would have been foolish not to do this. If an innovation's ultimate users do not buy into an idea, even if forced, they will kill it out of spite and to protect their turf. No one, particularly the most gifted operators, wants to be branded as a dinosaur. The best operators always seek an edge. I'd seek them out. In return, they looked carefully at whatever ideas I had brought them.

The only way to make the adaptation of a new product or idea work was to make it their idea. I was just the humble "tee up" guy. I made sure that they got the credit and the company celebrated them for their innovative approaches. When victories occurred, we had a parade and the operators marched up the company's equivalent of Main Street. Leadership applauded them for being thought leaders. Everyone won.

Not surprisingly, my success rate was very high when I took opportunities to new-deal approval committees with the active support of affected operators. These operators were going out on a limb and taking responsibility for making it work. The approval committees knew that if the operators were pitching a deal, the vetting process had been very thorough. Given these dynamics, companies often rushed to approve these operator-endorsed deals.

Large companies consist of individual fiefdoms that are fiercely protective of their turf and in most cases very conservative— "conservative" meaning they fight change imposed on their territories. They have good reasons for this orientation. Their business lines are very complex organisms. I like to describe them as big, beautiful, ornate machines. Tinkering with a well-oiled machine can be catastrophic. Don't fix it if it's not broken.

The managers in charge and operating these businesses had painstakingly organized their processes, technologies, and people to optimize performance. They had staffed their teams with knowledgeable professionals filling specific roles. Operators love their machines. They marvel at their efficiency. They love to tweak and polish them up. They know everything about everything in their realm. They are the rulers of their worlds. They have everything set up to run smoothly and well.

The last thing operators wanted was for a strategy guy like me to wander into their offices with a 30-year-old, freshly minted MBA suggesting there might be a better way. The operators' job is to protect and perfect their "machines," in part by keeping people like me out. A critical aspect of the operators' job is to reduce risk. They know 10 times more about the pieces of their puzzles than I do. And the downside is way worse than the upside. Seeing me, they'd pose cynical but pointed questions: "Sure, why shouldn't we put the company at risk to install an unproven idea that may or may not work? Why not disrupt the whole process we've spent years painstakingly building just to see what happens? Who loses if the idea fails?" And/or "Who will be there under a cloud cleaning up the mess?" The answers to these types of questions were obvious.

So my methodology was to find and initially vet disruptive companies with promising business models and then to run them through the gauntlet to see if they could come out the other end. Most didn't. The operators killed them, sometimes gleefully.

There was a method to my madness. Operators drove the vetting process. Working in sync with them, I would learn about and sometimes help develop their strategies. Having the operators define their priorities and target areas for improvement informed how I screened opportunities for review. With better screening came better candidates. The vetting process became a virtuous circle built on trust and mutual respect—a variant of the Golden Rule principle. I was on their side. We were at the table together, working to try to solve problems they had identified. Inclusion made all the difference.

As I said, operators ran prospective acquisitions through our evaluation gauntlet. They did so with the understanding that some opportunities must succeed or there'd be no need to screen any ideas or deals. Operators got to see new ideas for solving their problems (a real benefit). In exchange, they agreed to find a way to work with a certain percentage of these ideas. They couldn't always say "no." Otherwise, I would have to shut off the supply. It wasn't worth anyone's time to evaluate opportunities with no intention of approving any of them. That type of masquerading hurts reputations. The market would begin to see our company as rigid and closed-minded, unable to adapt to change.

I did have the leverage to shut down the flow of new ideas due to overly provincial parts of the organizations in which I worked. Change resistors got labeled as recalcitrant, stuck-in-the-mud operators. No one wanted that label. To be perceived as someone who couldn't consider new ideas was a career-ender.

As illustrated above, there is a delicate balance between old and new when introducing innovation into large, complex organizations. It's a form of détente diplomacy. Include the ultimate end users up front, have them lead the vetting process, pick your spots, fight if you have to but avoid fights if you can, and understand it's a numbers game. Rightfully, core businesses can reject most but not all opportunities. A few deals have to make it through to support effective innovation. That's the way it should be.

Back to Picassos in the attic. It is easier to recast existing ideas from inside the company than to bring new ideas from external sources. As I mentioned earlier, most answers to problems are within us. That applies to companies as well as human beings. These answers in the form of actual assets, materials, and know-how are scattered throughout a company. I became particularly good at finding the new in the old. Cinderella stories abound.

The advantage of recasting opportunities from within the company walls is that the opportunities are already a part of the enterprise. They're in. That fight for their existence has already been won. The opportunities are domestic, not foreign. They are neglected concepts, technologies, and methodologies that need to be shined up, recast, repositioned, and then ready to transform the world.

My role and innate curiosity propelled the exploration process forward. Sometimes a loyal protector understood an asset's potential but either lacked the influence to bring it forward or deliberately hid or undersold it. I helped articulate the story and find the right time and audience for its debut. Often this required finding and engaging an asset's loyal protector. I would persuade these caretakers hidden in the corporate woods that now was the time to reintroduce their once shiny object to company leadership. Realizing potential can be daunting, but it is impossible to move forward without taking risks.

Finding hidden gems was a constant throughout my career. At McKinsey, my job often centered on finding new uses for old products. At *National Geographic*, I searched for ignored content niches that could be expanded upon to grow into new businesses. I also helped to create new configurations of our existing published products for foreign markets. Same stuff, presented differently in different places to different audiences, sometimes with surprisingly positive results.

Searching for hidden gems followed me into healthcare. At Tenet, I found an entrepreneurial visionary, David Ricker, buried deep in the bowels of our purchasing group, Buy Power. David explained to me that we could market Tenet's massive purchasing inventory of medical items (everything from bedpans to IV poles) to other health systems and use our collective bargaining power to drive prices down. Buy Power ultimately became Broadlane, a very successful group purchasing organization.

As Buy Power mastered commodity purchases, we extended our collective approach to higher-cost, less routine items such as physician preference items (e.g., implants) and specialty surgery tools. We combined better prices with just-in-time delivery to lower storage and inventory costs. Win-win.

Tenet wanted more. We applied this collective purchasing approach aggressively to new businesses, including temporary staffing and contract nurses. We initiated a labor exchange to help lower staffing costs, which represent more than half of a typical hospital's expenses. In a short time, Buy Power grew from $1.7 billion in purchases to over $10 billion. Through Buy Power's increased buying power, Tenet not only reduced the prices it paid for products, it launched a successful new company built on an existing core function.

Tenet was basically a roll-up company initially run and controlled by financial engineers. They would buy hospital assets with debt until they could achieve maximum scale. Then they would unleash their marauding operators on the acquired companies. Like mercenaries, these operators were relentless. They applied tough cost cutting to increase organizational cash flow and profits. The process was relentless and effective. Three yards and a cloud of dust.

As Tenet acquired hospitals, I exercised my strategy privileges and sorted through their assets looking for hidden gems. Many of these hospitals contained nursing schools. Opportunity knocks. At that time, there was a huge nursing shortage. I did some research on what attracted nurses to specific hospitals. Education was at the top of the list. So we consolidated the schools, branded them, and bought a nursing digital education distribution platform. We distributed knowledge and credits from these previously ignored schools to Tenet's entire population of 50,000 nurses.

Tenet then, mistakenly in my view, sold the nursing school assets. The sales price was attractive because the schools supplied nurses to a desperate marketplace. Longer term, keeping the schools would have been more accretive to Tenet. The company had four schools at the time of its sale. Instead of selling, Tenet could have created a for-profit nursing school juggernaut. It would have been a highly profitable endeavor that also would have supplied nurses to Tenet—two benefits for the price of one. Oh well.

While at Tenet, I hired a former direct marketing colleague who was a consumer data expert. I had him review our hospitals' data streams. He enhanced this data set by combining it with external consumer data. Taken together, we had the beginnings of a large data platform that could predict patients' future health events and outcomes. We used this data platform to assemble a list of our hospitals' patients at risk for significant follow-on health events and dramatically cut these patients' subsequent treatment costs. New businesses associated with these analytics generated returns as high as 20 times and prevented numerous acute care episodes.

We then turned our analytical lens on Tenet's 50,000+ nurse and ancillary clinician population. We used data-driven insights to enhance the company's recruitment and retention tools. More successful recruiting and lower clinical staff turnover followed. Data analytics enabled us to understand and respond to the needs, wants, and desires of our clinical workforce. Information properly applied truly is powerful.

My Picassos-in-the-attic proclivity followed me from Tenet to Humana. Humana had an incredibly rich but woefully underutilized and siloed data pool. The health insurer paid for almost all of its members' health costs, so it had robust treatment protocol and outcome data at its fingertips. However, the company had not mined this rich trove of valuable clinical and claims data, nor built algorithms to predict individual health outcomes. The potential to discover diagnostic and care management insights by unifying, scrubbing, and integrating this data was enormous.

Seeing this opportunity, we did two things. We attacked the data itself by acquiring two companies to clean, homogenize, and analyze our data in real time. In sifting through the data, the analytics company generated clinical alerts that indicated where our members had incomplete profiles and care gaps. Addressing these "gaps in care" with our members enabled us to reduce their risks of catastrophic health events. Beyond eliminating care gaps, Humana built clinical algorithms and developed provider relationships to predict members at risk of acute episodes and proactively intervene to prevent them from happening.

By preventing acute episodes and related hospitalizations, Humana both improved its members' health and reduced its own medical loss ratio (the percentage of premium dollars spent for treatment). There are no better win-win outcomes in healthcare.

At Humana, our members expressed their strong desire to receive care in their homes. Examining the costs and outcomes of home-based care programs revealed massive opportunities to eliminate harm, accelerate healing, and enhance member satisfaction with our services. By investing in their home-based care and safety programs, we reduced hospital visits and enabled our fragile members to successfully "age in place." For example, we launched a home care coordination effort in Florida and supported it by buying a small home health company. This expanded our ability to care for our sickest members in their homes. The results were amazing. Humana's success in home-based care delivery is what subsequently triggered my interest in becoming Amedisys's CEO.

Did Humana crack the care code and discover all the secrets to value-based care provision? No way! We started on what is and will be a long, constant journey helping our members manage chronic illness. Are these the right initial steps? I think so. We'll know for sure when we assess longer term how these strategies affect member health and well-being. The challenge for Humana as a publicly traded company will be balancing its desire to develop paradigm-shifting population healthcare models with market demands for immediate financial returns. Humana has all the ingredients to become a transformative health company. I'm hopeful that it will find the motivation and courage to be one.

In its business models, the publishing industry assesses the lifetime value of its customers. Healthcare not so much. Lifetime value is a simple concept. It assesses and seeks to maximize how much customers will spend on companies' products and services over their lifetimes. For example, publishers predict how long customers will subscribe to their periodicals and invest in strategies that extend those consumer relationships. Taking a similar "lifetime value" approach should be a no-brainer in the health insurance business, where companies take financial risk on patient outcomes over a long period of time. Enhancing member health should be in the long-term interests of health insurers. In that sense, lifetime value is the perfect economic measure of success. That health insurers are just starting to measure lifetime value speaks to the industry's perverse economic incentives.

The ubiquity of lifetime value within the cultures of publishing companies made it easier to develop long-term customer relationships. We avoided transactional "one-and-done" sales strategies. To build enduring customer relationships, publishing companies invested more up front to cultivate customer loyalty. In publishing, we knew that the longer relationships lasted, the more enriching they would be to customers and the more profitable they would be to us. Why? Because over time the care and maintenance of longtime customers decreases. Publisher and clients learn to know and trust one another. Satisfying their needs leads loyal customers to purchase more products and services. It's no surprise, for example, that fans of *National Geographic* enjoy taking tours led by the company's content experts and buying travel products used and endorsed by these experts.

My favorite business book is Fred Reichheld's *The Loyalty Effect*. By dissecting the economic benefits of loyalty, Reichheld takes the concept of lifetime value to another level. Healthcare needs to embrace this theory. Given the high levels of chronic disease in America, companies that connect with and stick with their patients/members over the longer term have the capacity to improve their lifestyle decision-making and enhance their well-being. Imagine the loyalty effect that approach could generate in customer relationships!

Like Humana and Tenet, Amedisys started with data to understand how we could better engage with our employees, take better care of our patients, and deliver better outcomes. We realized that happier employees are essential to our success. They go the extra mile for our patients, stay with the company longer, and contribute their best thinking to our collective efforts to improve Amedisys's products and services.

Amedisys was not good at designing software, so we stopped trying to be. When I joined Amedisys as its CEO in 2014, there were lots of other things we weren't good at doing. Under my leadership, we stopped doing the things we were not good at and used the found energy and resources for the essential investments and activities we required to deliver superior home care services to our patients.

Lots of things we thought were integral to great care delivery weren't. So we stopped doing them, particularly if we were trying to do them on our own and failing. We mapped our business systems to assess how we delivered care from beginning to end. We then determined what skills and competencies were so important that we needed to do them ourselves, as well as what activities we could assign to outside partners and contractors as part of our holistic care delivery platform. Generating the best care outcomes and client experiences determined whether and when Amedisys owned, partnered, or contracted for service provision.

When I arrived, Amedisys was pushing too many back-office functions to its care centers. Most were not good at these functions, and ultimately it wasn't important if they were. So we started taking things off the plate of our care centers. We still are. Decentralized companies like Amedisys should only focus on doing the essentials well at the points where the company interacts with its customers (as Amedisys endeavors to do with our patients).

Less equals more. The fewer items on which companies focus, the better they will do on the things that do matter. That's why finding ways to centralize non-customer-facing functions is the best way to free care centers so they can focus all their attention on driving better clinical care and outcomes. This is where larger home care companies have distinct advantages over smaller providers. Centralizing coding, receivables management, contract negotiations, patient intake, legal services, and M&A builds cost-effective expertise and scale that optimize the competitive positioning of the company's care centers.

There is an interesting strategy book titled *The Discipline of Market Leaders* by Michael Treacy and Fred Wiersma. The authors advocate that narrowly focusing on a company's core group of customers and meeting their needs with intense operational focus will drive the best results. This approach unearths new opportunities to serve a company's most important clients more comprehensively and effectively. The moral of the strategy here is for companies to identify their best customers, drive operations to best meet their needs, and be alert to new service opportunities as they manifest themselves.

Recall Figure 6.1 showing the Horn of Plenty from Chapter 6. This simple visual depicts how businesses build off their core strategies. Success starts by excelling at the core businesses. Success expands by excelling at businesses that are skip-steps away from the core.

Adjacencies follow from there. It is essential to never lose focus on core business operations. Excel at the core before migrating to adjacent activities. Doing so too early is a risk.

Using the Horn of Plenty as our strategic guide was the key to Amedisys's seemingly remarkable success. We excelled at our core home care business before expanding into related service lines. When we were ready, these close-to-core moves mitigated risk and enhanced operations. By narrowing our focus, we redoubled our efforts in a few places that had organization buy-in. This narrowed focus shaped our incubation, M&A, and partnership strategies. We ignored any activities not encompassed within our Horn. This approach enabled appropriate expansion with less risk, more focus, and more buy-in (see Figure 9.1).

Another standard slide in my PowerPoint presentations describes the S-curve. First described in Chapter 5, the S-curve very clearly shows how today's business cannot sustain a company's operations tomorrow. At some point, companies have to pack up their tents and leave for greener pastures. The alternative is to tighten your belt and prepare to survive within a crowded and commoditized marketplace with lean competitors.

The nature of business is evolutionary and predatory. Entrepreneurs struggle to start something new. Initial market acceptance comes as the product adapts to customer need. Early adopters prove the business concept works. As the company's product moves into the mainstream, new competitors emerge even as the company thrives and grows fast. Barriers to entry weaken, and barbarian competitors hurtle into the marketplace. New innovators are solving issues that frustrate a now established company. At that point, it's time to evolve or lose competitive differentiation. Efficiency improvements can only capture a fraction of the margin the company generated when its product was unique. Jump the curve or die. This is the

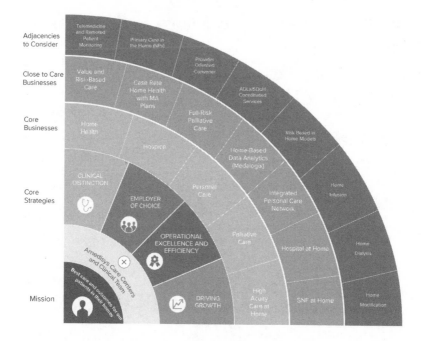

Core Strategies

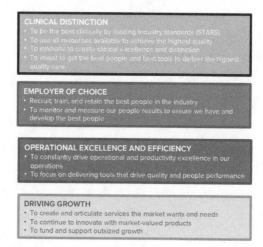

FIGURE 9.1 Using a Horn of Plenty approach to strategy, Amedisys built from its core outward, diversified its business offerings, turbocharged growth, and became the home care industry leader.

life of corporate progression in a single paragraph. It's tough in competitive free markets. It should be.

Innovation and new-product development require subsidies from core products when they're in their prime. Balancing current operations with new investments is among the hardest things to do in business. Companies that do it well become industry leaders. Evolution and change are constants. Businesses are born, grow, thrive, mature, and die. Are there exceptions and miracles? Yes, but they are like unicorns, very rare. If you're going to beat the odds, pay homage to the economic laws of nature and act accordingly.

KEY TAKEAWAYS

- Use whatever experiences you have. There are underlying rules and experiences that universally apply across businesses and industry sectors. This is why diversity of work experience can be so valuable. It provides perspective that those with singular work experience often lack.
- Innovation within large, complex organizations is hard but necessary. To drive change, leaders must work within the system and convert the organization's gatekeepers to take some risk. The best way to convert gatekeepers into change advocates is to invite them into the innovation dialogue early, earn their trust, respect their insights, and share the initiative's ownership with them.
- Shooting straight requires firing while standing on solid ground. Solid ground is the company's core business, what it's meant to do. The strategic "bullets" that leaders shoot emanate from the core and speed the company toward the future.

- Innovation can occur internally and externally, although gaining traction with externally generated innovations is more difficult. Internal innovations are easier to launch and manage and have higher success rates if they have buy-in from the company's stakeholders. Broader participation in organizational strategy works.

- Opportunity is everywhere. Good assets sometimes lose their luster. Take stock of assets as they fall out of favor. What is old and tired can become new and fresh with a bit of a "spit and polish." Good ideas are never really bad. They often get introduced at the wrong time and/or never catch fire for the wrong reasons.

- Make time to listen to new ideas. Be open to challenges and disruption. The future is full of surprises and turmoil. Being an intellectually curious leader gives a company a fighting chance of participating in that future, not being overwhelmed by it.

- All answers to a company's strategic challenges lie within the organization. To find them, leaders must cultivate an open and engaging operating culture. Finding solutions within the organization is beneficial in two ways. The company gets the right solution to a thorny challenge. Plus, employees demonstrate to themselves and the outside world that they have the depth and wherewithal to build, shape, and participate in the company's future.

CONCLUSION

One Final Road Trip

I decided to leave my position as CEO of Amedisys at the end of my seventh year while continuing to serve as its board chair. Maybe it was the seven-year itch, but it was probably more. Being honest with myself, I thought the organization needed fresh eyes and new energy. This meant applying the "cold eye" to myself.

A new leader could potentially see new paths and lead Amedisys into the future better than I could. The board asked for six months to transition the company to my successor. To minimize disruption, I completed most of my formal work prior to the announcement of my departure. I wanted to take my last two months as Amedisys's CEO to tour care centers, bear witness, and accompany caregivers on patient visits. I wanted to thank our caregivers again and again for the remarkable work they do every day with our patients, 65,000 times a day.

I felt this was the best way to leave what had for me been an incredible journey, one that had changed me and the company.

Building the best organization possible to serve the truly vulnerable and needy was an accomplishment for which we could all be justifiably proud. I wanted to thank as many people as I could in person for everything they did for our patients and for each other. I wanted to leave Amedisys with as strong an understanding as I could have of the people power that had driven our company to such unanticipated success. I wanted to reinforce my belief throughout the company and the industry that Amedisys's soul and success begins and ends with our caregivers and our patients.

In consultation with our clinical leaders, I mapped out a trip. They alerted everyone that I was coming. As usual with the best laid plans, they fell apart. I grabbed my car, which broke down twice, and hit the road. I had two months to visit as many care centers and caregivers as I could. I concentrated my travel in the South, where we have the most care centers. I ended up visiting 101 care centers in six states. I also visited another six in the Northeast prior to my Southern sojourn. My team created a humorous poster to commemorate my final road trip as CEO (Figure C.1).

I traveled several thousand miles and passed through close to a thousand towns. I slept in hotels, motels, B&Bs, and a guesthouse. The food was amazing and deliciously unhealthy. I had one lodging and eating rule—no chains. I stayed away from the Motel 6s and other common brands that are homogenizing and pudgifying America. Jane and Michael Stern's Roadfood website was my guide. I was up before dawn and arrived at my first care centers early enough for their morning reviews and check-ins. I took less-traveled "blue highways," a term coined by William Least Heat-Moon in his 1982 book *Blue Highways*. These are the back roads connecting out-of-the-way places; they are the small roads colored blue on Rand McNally's older maps.

Heat-Moon's book mimicked John Steinbeck's famous *Travels with Charley: In Search of America*, published in 1962. Steinbeck was

FIGURE C.1 Like Johnny Cash, I felt like "I'd been everywhere" on my last road trip as CEO. In departing, I wanted to emphasize that Amedisys's reason for being begins and ends with the compassionate care that our frontline staff provide to patients 65,000 times a day. It was my honor to honor them.

trying to find America's essence and so was Heat-Moon. Maybe I was too. I liked the idea that you could find a different, slower, and culturally richer America by getting off the interstate highways. There is a big difference. Travelers on the interstates reach their destinations faster but miss the local warmth and color that accompany slower, meandering journeys. I understood the interstate world too well. Traveling on back roads through rural America was a wonderful antidote to my harried executive life. I slowed down, got in the moment, and reveled in the company of frontline staff serving our patients in out-of-the-way places.

Aesthetically, care centers themselves are largely unimpressive, generally located in B-graded medical buildings or three-story office buildings. They're convenient for clinicians, who run in and out between patient visits for supplies and quick consultations and check-ins. We try to place our centers close to their referral sources. Being close to hospitals, physicians' offices, nursing homes, and medical office buildings is a priority.

Our offices were a mixed bag. Some were clean and spartan. Others were straight out of a calico crafts store. I had the performance statistics for each care center I visited but didn't need them. I could tell within 10 seconds of arriving whether a care center was a high performer. The great ones have a spirit that's apparent five steps into the room. Staff at these centers were collegial, celebratory, supportive, happy. They finished each other's sentences, loved each other's quirks, and celebrated each other's accomplishments. In many ways, they were a big extended family. By contrast, struggling centers were subdued, formal, and cautious. My years in the field had allowed me to develop a finely tuned anticipatory sense for instantly assessing a center's performance. One sniff and I knew whether a center was a strong, middling, or poor performer.

I was also able to go on patient visits where I observed and sometimes participated in delivering care. These visits were always reassuring to me. We consistently do good things for our patients.

Driving back toward Nashville on the Natchez Trace after a visit to Mississippi and northwest Alabama at the end of my tour, I had a chance to reflect on this final road trip. I had met with over a thousand caregivers, patients, and referral partners. Spring was in the air. There were daffodils along the highway. Colorful dogwood and redbuds were starting to blossom. There is nothing like the start of spring in the rural South.

My care center visits were inspiring. I sometimes tried to randomly drop into a center to surprise everyone, but word of my whereabouts spread like wildfire. Often centers staged welcoming parties, convened at the last minute, to say hello. My visits were mainly celebratory. I got lots of cool gifts and tchotchkes. The discussions generally stayed light, but we also delved into subjects concerning our business. The difficulty of hiring clinical staff, the consistent efforts of MA plans to commoditize our services, and the increasing complexity of our patients were frequent topics. These longstanding issues shape our caregivers' work lives but have very little to do with actual caregiving.

So what do we do? Like Arjuna, the warrior king in the *Bhagavad Gita*, we fight on—karma yoga—selfless action. We care and care and care and do so without selfishness. That's what I saw. It reconfirmed for me that we are a company of caregivers. As long as we understand this, Amedisys will be fine. Everything else follows from delivering great care. The more we focus on this, the better we will continue to do. The virtuous circle turns and turns. The more we see that the selfless action of caring is what we do, the better we will get at selfless caregiving. The crank pulls easier, and then you're there. That's the dream. If not us, then who?

Passing into Tennessee on that early spring evening, I saw a field I could not resist. It was full of daffodils. I pulled over and sat among the flowers. The air was heavy with their scent. The light was coming in beautifully slant as it does in early evening. It was the end of my trip.

As I sat there among the flowers, I realized what a blessing and a privilege it was for me to do the Amedisys work. I had found a place where I could give it my all, unadorned and unfiltered. Like the Fisher King in T. S. Eliot's "The Waste Land," there is a point where we must move on. The king has to die. New eyes, fresh energy, new blood must come in and guide the company to the next place. There is a finite time for leaders to be in place. I think America has it right with the presidency, eight years or two terms is enough. I had been the new energy, fresh eyes, and new blood, but now I wasn't. The last best thing you can do for something you love is to set it free. Hope that what we've built together lasts and gives the company enough solid ground to jump to the next stage.

I sat on the rise of the little hill full of blooming daffodils for quite a while. As dusk settled in, heavy clouds laden with pink and purple colors began to appear into the twilight.

Feeling conclusive and fulfilled, I got back in the car. I rolled down the windows, put on some opera music, turned the volume to full blast, and drove home to Nashville through the spring-scented night listening to Verdi's *La Bohème*.

AFTERWORD

Back into the Storm

Almost immediately after I retired as CEO of Amedisys, the company began to decline precipitously.

I received lots of advice about how to be a good ex-CEO. Since I remained board chair, I was intent on removing myself from day-to-day management responsibilities. No new CEO wants the old CEO hovering nearby. My board was particularly sensitive on this issue and advised me to give my successor a wide berth. Apparently, many thought I was a forceful and dominating presence. They didn't want my presence to limit my successor's ability to run the company.

I didn't believe this would be a problem. I was ready to retreat from the daily grind. I had worked closely with my replacement when he was Amedisys's Chief Operating Officer. No one wanted him to succeed more than I did. Besides, my successful leadership of Amedisys's turnaround had put me in another league professionally. An abundant number of interesting opportunities presented themselves to me. I wanted to test my theories on disruption and transformation within the healthcare industry. I wanted to engage as an investor and advisor with companies positioned to redefine health-care's brave new world. Plus, I had this book to write.

The post-COVID world and the isolation that occurred had a longer and more influential tail than many thought. COVID changed people's attitudes toward work, health, and lifestyle. The pandemic accelerated the shift of care delivery away from institu-tional settings. The high nursing home death rates from COVID and the draconian steps taken to prevent the spread of infection resulted in isolating existing residents and terrifying the public. Americans needing skilled nursing care searched for alternatives.

Home-based care offers an almost ideal solution to this dilemma. It avoids many of the problems that plague institutional care. It lim-its the spread of infectious disease. The setting is conducive to healing and human interaction. It offers warmth and comfort, not unfa-miliarity and isolation. When paired with telemedicine, home care becomes both more responsive and more efficient. Vulnerably ill peo-ple are safer. They avoid infection and receive personalized care deliv-ered via telemedicine and supplemented by in-person visits.

The stress on the system and those who were called on to deliver the care was considerable. It created significant healthcare labor shortages. Several factors contributed to the labor shortage. Demand for nursing services spiked after COVID landed on American shores. There were the additional protocols, documentation requirements, safety measures, and heightened personal health risks that burdened those providing care during the pandemic: the protective gear that people had to wear; the mechanics of intense infection control; the psychological toll of mounting disease and death; the lack of clear public health direction; uncertainty; and the fear, just to name a few. The US healthcare system was not prepared for these stresses and tee-tered on the brink of collapse. Caregiver burnout and deteriorating morale proliferated. A disproportionate share of healthcare workers, particularly in nursing, permanently left the workforce.

This phenomenon trickled down to Amedisys as I was transitioning to exit the company. We saw a significant increase in demand for our services (a good thing), but we did not have enough clinical staff, especially nurses, to meet the expanding demand. COVID-related burnout contributed to a spike in turnover that we had fought so hard to reduce. Higher turnover made our situation worse. We know how to engage and motivate nurses: Have great managers; make nurses feel part of a cohesive caregiving team; make them believe they are working for an organization that values great care, provides the best tools, and pays well. It became harder to achieve these objectives during the pandemic. Caregivers worked remotely under stress. They rarely saw their managers and coworkers. They could not visit locked-down care centers. As in the rest of the country, not all our employees agreed with mandated public health policies. Amedisys became the bad guy as we enforced the new rules. Often our nurses felt that the restrictions limited their ability to provide great patient care.

COVID vaccinations became a huge issue. Many who were against them wanted anonymity and didn't believe Amedisys had the right to know their vaccination status. Wage inflation for nurses hit the company like a freight train. A subsegment of the nursing population became mercenary: "If I'm risking my life to take care of infectious patients, I'm going to go to the place that pays me the most for the risk I'm taking."

Remote work was initially disruptive. More and more people wanted flexible work schedules. They resisted or outright revolted against working a regular 40-hour week in the office. While convenient, remote work is isolating and different. In response, Amedisys developed remote systems and management tools to coordinate care provision. It took some time for our people to adapt to the new and changed reality. As COVID dissipates, the Amedisys workforce wants greater flexibility and better work-life integration. These workers are less tolerant of traditional work strictures. The slow process of workforce reconfiguration in America has disrupted the industry's supply-demand dynamics. It will never be the same.

Like all personnel-heavy companies, Amedisys has taken its lumps during COVID and its aftermath. Delaying care for a rapidly aging, chronically ill population during COVID led to significant levels of unnecessary death. The crunch that providers are now experiencing is due, in part, to addressing the severe treatment needs of patients who did not seek or receive appropriate care during the pandemic. The nation's increasing levels of chronic illness and the debilitating nature of chronic diseases like cancer and diabetes have forced a landslide of cost and burden on the already stretched and sometimes broken US healthcare system.

The increasing growth of Medicare Advantage and the government's bumbling and blind increases to payers at the price of providers has created a consumer bias for Medicare-eligible Americans, those aged 65 or older. Enrollment in Medicare Advantage plans is growing at 8–10 percent annually while enrollment within original Medicare is actually declining. These dynamics have dramatically reduced profitability among already struggling home care providers. On average, Medicare Advantage plans pay about 60 percent of what traditional Medicare pays for home care services. When Medicare Advantage was a small part of Amedisys's business mix, we could afford the losses associated with servicing MA plan members. That is no longer true.

The MA plans pay us less, pay us late, and sometimes don't pay us at all. With Medicare Advantage plans growing so quickly, home care companies like Amedisys must receive higher payments for the services we provide or risk going out of business. Relative to CMS, most

Medicare Advantage plans are tougher, harder, and more difficult to do business with. Our losses are their profits. MA plans squeeze their suppliers, including home care providers, to offer their members more services and generate higher profits for themselves. Ironically, CMS has continued to cut home care payment rates even as it has granted substantially higher payments to MA plans. So companies like Amedisys that provide the needed home care services are getting it from both sides, falling revenues accompanied by higher expenses.

This pattern of events creates short-term disruption for home care providers even as longer-term trends support moving more and more healthcare into the home. Home care costs less. It's often more suitable for treating patients with chronic conditions. Best of all, consumers love it much more than institutionalized care. These basic tenets of home care remain true even as the turbulent current operating environment roils the sector.

Amedisys has not been immune from this market turmoil. The company failed to meet its own earnings guidance in 2022. Internally, Amedisys's operating character was diminishing. Before more damage occurred, the Amedisys board dismissed my successor and asked me to return to the company to stabilize and improve its performance. It's déjà vu all over again.

It's been a tough reentry. My team was not delighted to have me back. We had parted, and I had moved on. I did not want to have to write this Redux chapter, but here we are. "Redux" means "bring back" in Latin.

The value of Amedisys's stock had dropped by half since my departure as CEO. In my conversations with financial analysts covering the company, there was a general feeling that Amedisys had quickly lost its leadership position in key markets and services. Even some of the company's core areas of strength in patient care were deteriorating.

When chaos is swirling all around leaders, they can't succumb to it. They need to find a few key areas on which to focus. These areas should be ones that reestablish the company's true identity, that reinforce its reason for being, that inspire its employees to stand up and fight for its success. Amedisys's core tenets had not changed. Patients, our people, and our great tools are what distinguishes the company. When we get back to basics, we'll grow.

There are four things that Amedisys needs to do to get back on track. The first thing relates to turnover. Turnover has gone up, and it needs to come down. COVID has done a number on clinical professionals, especially nurses. There has been tremendous disillusionment within their ranks. Many felt exploited by their employers. Regulators have made their jobs more difficult. Thousands died from COVID. Too many have not liked what they've seen and are leaving the profession. They're often trading frontline caregiving for less skilled positions, sometimes even driving for Uber. These work pressures along with significant wage pressure requires Amedisys to reestablish why the company is different and why our clinicians should commit to us for the long term. Not easy to do but absolutely necessary. Amedisys is only as good as the care its frontline providers deliver. Full stop.

Second, Amedisys has to increase the payments it receives for providing home care services to members of Medicare Advantage health plans. Negotiating with commercial payers is difficult and complex. If the payment model doesn't work for efficient and effective providers like Amedisys, then it won't work long term for the MA plans. We are working hard to migrate MA plans to value-based payment models where we share in the financial benefits of delivering superior care outcomes, reducing hospitals visits, and improving star ratings (theirs and ours).

Third, we need to centralize care center activities that do not create direct value with our patients and frontline caregivers. These "back-office functions," such as billings, receivables management, compliance, and HR, are essential but lend themselves to centralization. Freeing our 550 care centers of back-office responsibilities enables them to focus solely on enriching the work lives of our caregivers and delivering unparalleled high-quality patient care.

Fourth and last, Amedisys has to optimize its investment in Contessa. We made a bold bet in buying Contessa. We now have to scale it and make it an ongoing profitable enterprise. Our hypothesis is that hospital-at-home care, SNF-at-home care, and at-home palliative care not only are viable businesses but represent the future cornerstones of value-based care delivery. It's not enough just to believe this; we need to prove it. That means enhancing Contessa's service offerings, improving their efficiency, *and* expanding the client base. This will be exciting work. Contessa's fundamentals are solid. They are working well now on a relatively small client base. Imagine their impact and profitability at scale.

These four area of focus are the right ones. They have the highest ability to drive our business forward. The key now is to break these four broad areas into their component parts with tangible goals for each. We'll ask our people responsible for execution to help us complete that task and design implementation plans. As this unfolds, we'll rigorously review progress, honestly assess our performance, solve problems quickly, remove obstacles as necessary, and tweak execution strategies when we fall behind.

Big-bang actions rarely accomplish anything of substance. Manageable change is hard-won and incremental. It's accomplished by breaking big tasks into doable pieces, achieving regular small victories and occasional big ones. It takes persistence. Rarely discourage and always pushing, CEOs must rise to the challenge every day, achieving successes bit by bit. It's a long, arduous, and yet enjoyable endeavor once things get moving.

If these mechanics don't sound familiar, then you have not been reading this book carefully. Getting the right people on task, setting the right priorities, and driving continuous performance improvement are the keys to operational excellence. The Golden Rule, loyalty economics, the Horn of Plenty, and S-curve strategies all have to come together to achieve greatness. It is within the people of Amedisys to make greatness happen.

The people on the team have dug in, as I knew they would. They have done it before and will do it again. Will we need some new horses? Absolutely. When leaders crest the mountaintop and survey the new "territory ahead," their on-the-spot assessments reveal gaps. Like a contractor with a fresh remodeling plan, I'm going to need some outside "wall busters" to mix in with my team. Together, we'll push the pace, not get hung up by old thinking, past assumptions, and unnecessary hand-wringing. We'll get there. No doubt. But it will be painful at times.

At the same time, I know I have to go sooner rather than later. Beyond the short-term repair period, I'm not the right person to lead Amedisys forward. I'm a temporary safety blanket plugged in to hold things together while we look for the next leader. I think I know how Lazarus felt when summoned from the dead. I devoted much of my time at Oxford to studying the work of T. S. Eliot. Eliot begins his epic poem "The Waste Land" with these lines:

> April is the cruellest month, breeding
> Lilacs out of the dead land, mixing
> Memory and desire, stirring
> Dull roots with spring rain.

Rebirth is brutal and disruptive. Like Eliot says, the old king has to die for the new king to ascend to the throne. As they have said for centuries in England, "The King (or Queen) is dead. Long live the King." Unimpeded by the old king's legacy, the new king can move the nation forward. I know this to be true for me and Amedisys. The best thing I can give this company that I love and have worked so hard to restore, rewire, and reimagine is the freedom to move forward unabated by my influence.

I have explained this to the members of my board, and they have reluctantly acknowledged this truth. As I write, Amedisys has just announced that Richard Ashworth, the former president of Walgreens and CEO of Tivity, will become the new CEO. It's Richard's time to take the baton and run up the next mountain. Amedisys needs fresh eyes, new perspectives, and new energy to get to a higher place. I know he'll be a great CEO.

These are exactly my sentiments. All leaders should make an equivalent pledge to their companies.

Has Amedisys become a better company than when I took the CEO reins in 2014? Unquestionably so. Knowing when to go is a tough call, but getting the departure timing right is among a CEO's most important responsibilities. Too many CEOs stay well past their "sell by" date. It is an ignoble way to finish.

Plus, I'm not done. I want to tackle a new set of problems, align with a fresh group of team members, set the course, and get to work. As karma yoga teaches, selfless work done for the sake of work itself is the way to enlightenment. That's my journey. I wish you well on yours too and hope my story and observations have been helpful to you. There are no final destinations, just marvelous journeys. Ultimately, it is the fights, the joys, the agonies, the hard lessons, and the gumption to stay in the game that make our individual journeys worthwhile. Godspeed, and may your journey be a worthy one.

ACKNOWLEDGMENTS

I offer these acknowledgments with enormous gratitude.

For my intrepid partner and compassionate and wise wife, Serena, and my loving and constantly illuminating daughters—Maude, Marina, and Francesca. Thank you for putting up with me. You were dealt a challenging hand.

For my mom, who taught me grit and persistence. For my brother and sister, Karl and Adrie, for their support and love along the journey.

For David Johnson, my former colleague and patient editor. This book would never have been published without his encouragement, guidance, and insightful pen. And Casey Ebro, at McGraw Hill, for taking this on and guiding it through.

In memory of and with appreciation for Bill Borne, the founder and former Chairman and CEO of Amedisys. Thank you for all you created and the good you did for Amedisys's patients over the 30+ years you led the company. It was a privilege to follow you.

For the Amedisys Board of Directors, present and past, who have provided me guidance and support—Julie Klapstein, Molly Coye, Terri Kline, Ivanetta Davis-Samuels, Vickie Capps, Jeff Rideout,

Bruce Perkins, Nat Zilkha, Don Washburn, David Pitts, Peter Ricchutti, Jake Netterville, and Linda Hall.

For my Amedisys team and colleagues, present and past, who have helped and guided me along the way—Scott Ginn, Nick Muscato, Mike North, Denise Bohnert, Kendall Hagood, Jennifer Guekert, Scott Levy, Adam Holton, Travis Messina, Tammy Pebbles-Forest, Dave Kemmerly, Chris Gerard, Sharon Brunecz, Dan McCoy, Steve Seim, Larry Parnosky, Megan Ambers, Susan Sender, Marty Howard, Kris Novak, Scott Holcomb, David Pearce, Ronnie LaBorde, Janine Jones, Tracey Waller, Kendra Kimmons, Cindy "Cha-Cha" Ciaccio, Teonie Aurelio, Geoff Abraskin, Anessa Johnson, Lynn Wilson, Phil Nalaboff, Keith Hambreck, Elizabeth Robinson, Regarner Thompson, Sandice Schrauf, Deana Wilson, and all the caregivers in the Amedisys family. What you do every day is heroic and purposeful. Godspeed to you all! Good luck Richard Ashworth!

For those who have helped and guided along the way— Trevor Fetter, Barry Schochet, Jeff Barbakow, David Ricker, Grant Wicklund, Keith Henthorne, Chuck O'Meara, Neil Borg, Mandar Vadhavkar, Sean Slovenski, Ralph Judah, Robb Vorhoff, Jon Kaplan, John Kao, Mike McCallister, Jim Murray, Ken Fasola, Bonnie Hathcock, Amed Ghouri, Raghu Sugavanam, Tom Corry, Adam Boehler, Bill Frist, Bryan Cressey, David Brailer, Jonathan Flicker, Julie Murchinson, Mike Pykosz, Namhee Han, Peter Gilhuly, John and Jill Walsh, Matt Larew, Sheryl Skolnick, Brian Tanquilut, Keith Myers, April Anthony, Alex Drane, Shuja Ali, Ian Sacks, David Tamburri, Kate Ross, Paul Schulz, Bob Attiyeh, Russ Thomas, Chris Meade, David Jones, Eric Larsen, Frank Williams, Robert Musslewhite, Martin Coulter, Charles Beckman, Greg Price, Chris Toderoff, Alan Wheatley, George Renaudin, Brian Morfitt, Ben Magnano, Brad Fleugel, Ted Riehle, Raun Thorpe, Brian Tichenor,

Jim Waldrop, Will Gray, Eddy Farmer, John Tomasi, Will Rogers, Grant McCargo, Robert Lair, Nicola Knipe, Rick Soloman, Donnelley and Cindy Erdman, Teresa McWilliams, and Fred Reichheld.

As stated in the Introduction, all profits of this book go to the Amedisys Foundation, a not-for-profit established to help our Amedisys caregivers, as well as our patients and their families, in times of extraordinary need.

INDEX

Department of Justice (DOJ), 7–8
Director of operations (DOO),
  66–70, 86–88
The Discipline of Market Leaders
  (Treacy and Wiersma), 153
Displaced employees (*see* Departing
  employees)
Diversification, 120, 136–137
Diversity, of work experiences, 156
Dividends, 116
DOJ (Department of Justice),
  7–8
DOO (director of operations),
  66–70, 86–88
Duckworth, Angela, 25–26

Earnings before interest, taxes,
  depreciation, and amortization
  (EBITDA), xvi, 86–87, 123,
  127
EBITDA multiple, 127
Education, 21–24
Electronic medical records (EMRs),
  67–68
Elements of Style (Strunk and
  White), xxii
Eliot, T. S., 164, 172
Employer of Choice, xvi
Empowerment, 75
EMRs (electronic medical records),
  67–68
Enterprise view of corporate
  officers, 64
Epic of Gilgamesh, 59
Europe, 21
Examination, in turnaround stage,
  101–102
Experimentation, 136

Failure, 101–102, 136
Farmer, Eddy, 17, 18
Farmer, Mrs., 17–18
Fear, 20

Feedback:
  in culture of trust, 65, 77
  from frontline operations, 37
  learning from, 51, 52
  soliciting, on walkabout, 42–44
  structures for receiving, 66
  in turnaround stage, 99–100,
    109
Fee-for-service plans, 128
Fetter, Trevor, xvii, xviii
Finance team, in flood response,
  57–58
Fired employees (*see* Departing
  employees)
Florida, 90, 125, 150
Focus:
  on care delivery, 63–64, 96,
    102–103, 152–153
  of leaders, 169–170
  narrowing of operational, 96,
    153–154
  in turnaround stage, 111
Former employees, relationships
  with, 34–36
Founder-run companies, 48–50,
  53–54
Fraud, 82–83, 117, 124
Frontline employees and operations:
  amplifying voices of, 77
  AMS3 testing at, 30
  corporate function in service of,
    48
  learning from, 51
  post-flood field visits with, 56–57
  primacy of, 64
  visits to, 40–48, 159–164
  (See also specific types of employees)
Fullbright Fellowship, 24
Funding, investment, 123

Gatekeepers, 156
Gates, Bill, 22
General Electric (GE), 21

ABOUT THE AUTHOR

PAUL KUSSEROW is Chairman and former CEO of Amedisys, a publicly traded company and leading provider of home health, hospice, palliative care, personal care, and high-acuity care services, with over 22,000 employees in 39 states and the District of Columbia, making over 12.3 million patient visits per year.

A healthcare veteran with 25 years of experience driving growth strategies, Kusserow served as Chairman of the Board of Amedisys prior to his return as CEO. From 2014 to early 2022, he was President and CEO of the company, which grew tenfold under his leadership. His hands-on involvement helped raise Amedisys in the ranks of home healthcare, moving from 3.2 stars to 4.6-star reviews. He is widely recognized as a thought leader and industry innovator.

Prior to joining Amedisys, Kusserow served in successive roles as President and Vice Chairman of Alignment Healthcare, Inc., an integrated clinical care company focused on providing care to the Medicare population; SVP and Chief Strategy, Innovations, and Corporate Development Officer of Humana, Inc., a Fortune 75 healthcare services and benefits company; and SVP of Strategy and

Ventures at Tenet Healthcare, a Fortune 500 hospital and ambulatory surgery company.

He is on the boards of Oak Street Health (NYSE: OSH); PurFoods, a medical and nutritional food company; Matrix Medical Network, a Medicare risk-assessed company; HealthPilot, a digitized Medicare enrollment company; and Scion, a hospital and LTACH company. He previously served on the boards of Connecture (Nasdaq: CNRX), New Century Health, Picwell, and Availity where he served as board chair. Kusserow started his career as a management consultant at McKinsey and Company.

He received his bachelor of arts from Wesleyan University, where he was a member of Phi Beta Kappa, an Olin Fellow, a Brown Scholar, and a Student Fellow at the Center for the Humanities. He received his master of arts from Oxford University, where he was a Rhodes Scholar.